Collins | English for Exams

Cambridge English Qualifications

A2 KEY

8 practice tests

Published by Collins
An imprint of HarperCollins Publishers
Westerhill Road
Bishopbriggs
Glasgow
G64 2QT

HarperCollins Publishers
Macken House,
39/40 Mayor Street Upper,
Dublin 1
D01 C9W8

Second edition 2020

10 9 8 7 6 5 4

© HarperCollins Publishers 2014, 2020

ISBN 978-0-00-836749-7

Collins® and COBUILD® are registered trademarks of
HarperCollins Publishers Limited

www.collins.co.uk/elt

MIX
Paper | Supporting
responsible forestry
FSC™ C007454
www.fsc.org

If you would like to comment on any aspect of this book,
please contact us at the given address or online.
E-mail: dictionaries@harpercollins.co.uk

facebook.com/collinselt

@CollinsELT

Authors: Sarah Jane Lewis and Patrick McMahon
Series editor: Celia Wigley
For the Publisher: Lisa Todd and Sheena Shanks
Editor: Anastasia Vassilatou
Typesetter: Jouve, India
Illustrations: Jouve, India
Photographs: Shutterstock.com
Printed and bound in the UK by
Ashford Colour Press Ltd.
Audio recorded and produced by ID Audio, London
Cover designer: Gordon McGilp
Cover illustration: Maria Herbert-Liew
Sample Answer sheets (pages 196–9): Reproduced
with permission of Cambridge Assessment English
© UCLES 2019

The Publishers gratefully acknowledge the permission
granted to reproduce the copyright material in this book.
Whilst every effort has been made to trace the copyright
holders, in cases where this has been unsuccessful, or if
any have inadvertently been overlooked, the Publishers
would gladly receive any information enabling them to
rectify any error or omission at the first opportunity.

All exam-style questions and sample answers in this
title were written by the authors.

About the authors

Sarah Jane Lewis is an experienced writer and editor
of primary and secondary course material with over
10 years' experience in the education publishing sector,
working with organisations across Europe, Asia and North
and South America. As well as working as a teacher of
academic and general English to young learners, teens
and adults in the UK and Greece, she also has experience
in preparing candidates for Cambridge English exams
and has a special interest in young learners and
assessment. She is the author of a variety of engaging
books and materials for young learners and young adults.

Patrick McMahon is a university lecturer, teacher
trainer, materials writer and academic. He has taught
English in universities, colleges, secondary schools
and language schools in the UK, mainland Europe, Asia
and the Middle East. He has written a broad range of
materials for publishers and specialises in English for
Academic Purposes.

Contents

How to use this book

Who is this book for?

This book will help you to prepare for the *Cambridge Assessment English A2 Key* exam. The exam is also known as the *KET* exam. The exam was updated for 2020 and this book was written for the new exam. This book will be useful if you are preparing for the exam for the first time or taking it again. The book has been designed so that you can use it to study on your own, however, you can also use it if you are preparing for the *A2 Key* exam in a class.

The book contains:

- **Tips for success** – important advice to help you to do well in the exam
- **About A2 Key** – a guide to the exam
- **How to prepare for the test** – advice to help you to succeed in each paper
- **Practice tests** – eight complete practice tests
- **Mini-dictionary** – definitions of the more difficult words from the practice tests
- **Audio scripts** – the texts of what you hear in the Listening and Speaking parts
- **Sample answer sheets** – make sure you know what the answer sheets look like
- **Answer key** – the answers for Reading and Listening
- **Model answers** – examples of good answers for the Writing and Speaking parts
- **Speaking: Additional practice by topic** – more sample questions to help you prepare for the Speaking test
- **Audio** – all the recordings for the practice tests as well as model answers for Speaking are available online at www.collins.co.uk/eltresources

Tips for success

- **Register for the test early** – If you are studying on your own, use the Cambridge Assessment English website to find your local exam centre. Register as early as you can to give yourself lots of time to prepare.
- **Start studying early** – The more you practise, the better your English will become. Give yourself at least two months to revise and complete all the practice tests in this book. Spend at least one hour a day studying.
- **Time yourself** when you do the practice tests. This will help you to feel more confident when you do the real exam.
- **Do every part** of each practice test. Don't be afraid to make notes in the book. For example, writing down the meaning of words you don't know on the page itself will help you to remember them later on.

Using the book for self-study

If you haven't studied for the *A2 Key* exam before, it is a good idea to do all the tests in this book in order. If you have a teacher or friend who can help you with your speaking and writing, that would be very useful. It is also a good idea to meet up with other students who are preparing for the exam or who want to improve their English. Having a study partner will help you to stay motivated. You can also help each other with areas of English you might find difficult.

Begin preparing for the *A2 Key* exam by getting to know the different parts of the exam, what each part tests and how many marks there are for each part. Use the information in the *About the A2 Key* section to find out all you can. You can also download the *A2 Key Handbook* from the Cambridge Assessment English website for more details.

You need to know how to prepare for each of the parts of the exam in the best way possible. The *How to prepare for the test* section in this book will be useful. Try to follow the advice as it will help you to develop the skills you need.

In the practice tests in this book, you will see certain words highlighted in grey. These are the more difficult words and you can find definitions of these in the *Mini-dictionary* at the back of the book. The definitions are from *Collins COBUILD* dictionaries. It's a good idea to download the *Cambridge A2 Key Vocabulary List* from the Cambridge Assessment English website. This is a list of words that you should understand at A2 level. Look through the list and make a note of the words you don't know. Then look up their meaning in a dictionary. You could use the *Collins COBUILD* online dictionary: www.collinsdictionary.com Knowing these words will help you to do better in the exam. Search 'A2 Key Vocabulary List 2020'.

Preparing for the Writing and Speaking parts

When you are ready to try the practice tests, make sure you answer the questions in the Writing parts as well as the Speaking parts. You can only improve your skills by practising a lot. Practise writing to a time limit. If you find this difficult at first, start by writing a very good answer of the correct length without worrying about time. Then try to complete your writing faster until you can write a good answer within the time limit. Learn to estimate the number of words you have written without counting them. Study the model answers at the back of the book. This will give you a clear idea of the standard your answers need to be. Don't try to memorise emails, notes or stories for the Writing part or answers to the questions in the Speaking part. If you work your way through the book, you should develop the skills and language you need to give good answers in the real exam.

The Speaking part in this book has accompanying audio so that you can practise answering the examiner's questions. You will be Candidate B, so if you hear the examiner ask Candidate B a question, this means you should answer by pausing the audio on your computer and answering the question. In Part 2 of the Speaking paper, you are expected to have a conversation with Candidate A. Again, you will be Candidate B and will respond to Candidate A's statements or questions. This experience will not be 100% authentic as Candidate A cannot respond to your statements or questions, however, this book and the audio have been designed to give you an excellent opportunity to practise answering questions through the eight practice tests. Once you have finished the Speaking part, you can listen to the model answers for Candidate B that have been provided for you. Another option is that you record your answers and then compare these with the model answers.

Please note that there are two versions of the Speaking Test audio:

- The first version contains the pauses for you to practise answering the questions in the Speaking tests. This is when you have to answer the questions for Candidate B. The scripts for this audio can be found from page 167 onwards in your book. For example, you'll see on page 169 that Test 1 Speaking audio track is labelled 'Track 06'. Look for Track 06 when you search for the audio online.

- The second version of the audio contains the Model Answers for the Speaking tests. These are for you to listen to, to see how a good student might answer the questions in the Speaking test. The scripts for this audio can be found from page 207 onwards in your book. You'll see that these audio files are labelled with an 'a' at the end, for example Track 06a, etc. Look for Track 06a when you search for the audio online.

At the back of the book you'll find more sample questions for the Speaking test. These provide another opportunity to practise answering questions that an examiner might ask you. There are 16 topics and all the questions have been recorded. Try answering these questions as fully as possible. Don't just give a 'yes/no' answer but try to give a reason or an example in your answer. Finally, read as much as possible in English; this is the best way to learn new vocabulary and improve your English.

About A2 Key

The *Cambridge A2 Key* exam is a pre-intermediate-level English exam delivered by Cambridge Assessment English. It is for students who need to show that they can deal with everyday English at a pre-intermediate level. In other words, you have to be able to:

- understand simple written information such as signs and notes
- write in simple English on everyday subjects
- show you can follow and understand a range of spoken materials such as announcements when people speak reasonably slowly
- show you can take part in different types of interactions using simple spoken English.

The exam is one of several offered by Cambridge Assessment English at different levels. The table below shows how *A2 Key* fits into the Cambridge English Qualifications. The level of this exam is described as being at A2 on the Common European Framework of Reference (CEFR).

	CEFR	Cambridge English Scale	Cambridge qualification
Proficient user	C2	200–230	C2 Proficiency (CPE)
	C1	180–199	C1 Advanced (CAE)
Independent user	B2	160–179	B2 First (FCE)
	B1	140–159	B1 Preliminary (PET)
Basic user	A2	120–139	A2 Key (KET)

The *A2 Key* qualification is for students studying general English or those students in higher education. It is an ideal first exam for those new to learning English and gives learners confidence to study for higher Cambridge English Qualifications. Cambridge Assessment English also offers an *A2 Key for Schools* qualification. Both tests use English in everyday situations. The only difference is that *Cambridge English: Key for Schools* is for candidates who are at school. If you are a school-age learner, it would be better for you to take the *A2 Key for Schools* test and use the *Collins Practice Tests for A2 Key for Schools* to prepare for the exam.

There are three papers (or tests) in *A2 Key*:

- Paper 1: Reading and Writing (1 hour)
- Paper 2: Listening (approximately 30 minutes)
- Paper 3: Speaking (8–10 minutes)

Timetabling

You take the Reading and Writing and Listening papers on the same day. You will take the Speaking test several days before or after the other papers. If you are studying on your own, you should contact your exam centre for dates. The exam is paper based. You can also take the exam on computer in some countries. For more information, see: https://www.cambridge-exams.ch/exams/CB_exams.php.

Paper/Test 1 Reading and Writing (1 hour)

Candidates need to be able to understand simple written information such as signs and newspapers and produce simple written English.

The **Reading and Writing** paper has seven parts. Reading parts 1–5 have 30 questions and there is one mark for each question. Writing parts 6 and 7 have only one question each. Students should spend about 40 minutes on the Reading parts and about 20 minutes on the Writing parts of this test.

The **Reading** section has five parts.

Part 1 has six short emails, notices, signs or text messages. There are three sentences next to each one. You have to choose which sentence matches the meaning of the email, notice, sign or text message. (Total marks: 6)

Part 2 has seven questions and three short texts on the same topic. You have to match each question to one of the texts. (Total marks: 7)

Part 3 has a longer text, for example, a simplified newspaper or magazine article. There are five multiple-choice questions with three options, A, B and C. (Total marks: 5)

Part 4 has a short text with six numbered spaces. You decide which of the three words provided belongs in each gap. (Total marks: 6)

Part 5 has a short text with six gaps. You have to fill in six gaps in a text or texts using single words. (Total marks: 6)

The **Writing** section has two parts: Parts 6 and 7 of the Reading and Writing paper.

In **Part 6**, you write a short email or note. This should be 25 words or more. (Total marks: 15)

In **Part 7**, you write a short story using picture prompts. This should be 35 words based on three picture prompts. (Total marks: 15)

In each part, marks are awarded in the following ways:
- five marks if you include all the necessary information
- five marks if you organise your message so a reader can follow it easily
- five marks if you use a good range of grammar structures and vocabulary.

Paper/Test 2 Listening (30 minutes)

Candidates need to show they can follow and understand a range of spoken materials, such as announcements, when people speak reasonably slowly.

The **Listening** paper has five parts and there are 25 questions in total.

Part 1 has five short dialogues, for example, conversations at home or in a shop, and five questions. For each question, you have to listen and choose the correct answer from three options: A, B or C. The options are pictures. (Total marks: 5)

Part 2 has a longer text. You listen and write the missing information (prices, times, telephone numbers) in the gaps. You should write only one word, or a number, or a date, or a time for your answer. (Total marks: 5)

Part 3 has a longer informal conversation. You listen and choose the correct answer to a question from three options: A, B or C. The questions include opinions and attitudes of the speaker. (Total marks: 5)

Part 4 has five short conversations. You listen and choose the best answer from the three options: A, B or C. (Total marks: 5)

Part 5 has a longer conversation between two people who know each other. You match each of five items in the first list with five of the eight items in the second list. (Total marks: 5)

Paper/Test 3 Speaking (8-10 minutes)

Candidates take the Speaking test with another candidate or in a group of three. They are tested on their ability to take part in different types of interaction: with the examiner, with the other candidate and by themselves.

The **Speaking** paper has two parts.

In **Part 1** the examiner asks you some questions about your name, where you live, your daily life, etc. and then the examiner asks you a longer 'Tell me something about ...' question. You respond to the examiner. (Time: 3–4 minutes)

In **Part 2**, the examiner gives you five pictures on a particular topic, e.g. hobbies. You talk together with the other student and discuss the activities, things or places in the pictures. After you have spoken for 1–2 minutes, the examiner continues the conversation by asking you questions related to the pictures. Then the examiner asks you two more questions on the same topic. (Time: 4–6 minutes)

Marks and results

After the exam, all candidates receive a Statement of Results. Candidates whose performance ranges between CEFR Levels A1 and B1 (Cambridge English Scale scores of 100–150) also receive a certificate.

The Statement of Results shows the candidate's:

- score on the Cambridge English Scale for their performance in each of the four language skills (reading, writing, listening and speaking).
- score on the Cambridge English Scale for their overall performance in the exam. This overall score is the average of their scores for the four skills.
- grade – this is based on the candidate's overall score.
- level on the CEFR – this is also based on the overall score.

The certificate shows the candidate's:

- score on the Cambridge English Scale for each of the four skills.
- overall score on the Cambridge English Scale.
- grade.
- level on the CEFR.
- level on the UK National Qualifications Framework (NQF).

For *A2 Key*, the following scores will be used to report results:

Cambridge English Scale Score	Grade	CEFR Level
140–150	A	B1
133–139	B	A2
120–132	C	A2
100–119	Level A1	A1

Grade A: Cambridge English Scale scores of 140–150

Candidates sometimes show ability beyond Level A2. If a candidate achieves a Grade A in their exam, they will receive the *Key English Test* certificate stating that they demonstrated ability at Level B1.

Grades B and C: Cambridge English Scale scores of 120–139

If a candidate achieves a Grade B or Grade C in their exam, they will receive the *Key English Test* certificate at Level A2.

CEFR Level A1: Cambridge English Scale scores of 100–119

If a candidate's performance is below Level A2, but falls within Level A1, they will receive a *Cambridge English* certificate stating that they demonstrated ability at Level A1.

Scores between 100 and 119 are also reported on your Statement of Results, but you will not receive a *Key English Test* certificate.

For more information on how the exam is marked, go to: http://www.cambridgeenglish.org

Working through the Practice Tests in this book will improve your exam skills, help you with timing for the exam, give you confidence and help you get a better result in the exam.

Good luck!

How to prepare for the test

Reading

» **READING CHALLENGE 1: 'I don't know a lot of the words that I see in the texts or in the questions.'**

SOLUTION: Build your vocabulary. Start by downloading the *Cambridge A2 Key Vocabulary List* from the Cambridge Assessment English website. This is a list of words that you should understand. Look through the list and make a note of the words you do not know. Then look up their meaning in a dictionary. If you know these words, you will do better in the exam.

SOLUTION: Use a learner's dictionary when you study. Dictionaries such as the *Collins COBUILD Intermediate Learner's Dictionary* have clear definitions, example sentences, information about grammar and illustrations to help you to build your vocabulary. At the back of this book, there is a *Mini-dictionary* with definitions of difficult words. The definitions come from Collins COBUILD dictionaries.

SOLUTION: Use 'key' words and phrases (e.g. *for instance, but*) that come before and after unknown words to help you guess their meaning. Read the sentence with the unknown word carefully. In the table below there are some ideas for how key words and phrases can help you to understand a word. The unknown word is underlined.

Guessing the meaning of unknown words		
Ideas	**Key words and phrases**	**Examples**
If you don't know a word, look for examples near the unknown word. If you understand the examples, you can use them to guess the meaning of the unknown word.	*such as* *including* *like* *for instance* *for example*	*We went on lots of different* <u>*excursions*</u>. **For instance**, *we went walking in the mountains, we visited a famous castle and we went on a boat trip.*
If you don't know a word, look for key words that show the writer is contrasting two ideas. The unknown word might have the opposite meaning to the idea in the sentence before or after it.	*but* *However, . . .* *Unlike X, Y . . .* *On the other hand, X . . .*	*They wanted to have the barbecue* <u>*outdoors*</u> **but** *it was raining so they had lunch inside the house.*

SOLUTION: Prefixes and suffixes can help you to guess the meaning of unknown words. A prefix is one or more letters, e.g. *un-, dis-*, that go at the beginning of a word, e.g. *unhappy, disorganised*. A suffix is one or more letters, e.g. *-ful, -ation, -y, -ment*, that go at the end of a word, e.g. *useful, enjoyment*. If you learn the meanings of common English prefixes and suffixes, you will be able to guess the meaning of many unknown words. For example, the prefixes *un-* and *dis-* give a word a negative meaning.

» **READING CHALLENGE 2: 'I need a long time to find all the answers in Parts 2 and 3.'**

SOLUTION: Read the text quickly using skimming and scanning skills to find the answers. Skimming is when you read a text quickly, paying attention only to the most important ideas. In this way, you can often quickly find the part that of the text that gives you the answer. This will save you a lot of time. In the table below there is some information on where to find important ideas.

Part of the text	Skimming strategy
Title	Read the title; this sometimes gives you an idea of what the text is about.
Introduction	Read the last one or two sentences of the introductory paragraph. They often include the main idea of the text.
Main paragraphs	Read the first and last sentence of a paragraph. They usually include the main idea of the paragraph.

Scanning is when you read a text quickly in order to find specific key words or ideas. After you have read a question, make a note of any key words or ideas such as names or numbers. Then scan the text, looking for those key words or ideas.

You do not need to understand every word when you skim or scan a text. The most important thing is to find the information you need in order to answer the questions quickly and correctly. To practise skimming and scanning, find an article in a newspaper or magazine. First, skim the article and write down the most important ideas on a piece of paper. Then scan it for key words or ideas such as names or numbers. The more you practise skimming and scanning, the better you will become, so try to practise every day.

SOLUTION: Time yourself when you do practice tests. You should not spend more than 40 minutes on Parts 1–5 of the Reading and Writing paper. While you work on the questions, make sure you look at your watch occasionally. Do not spend too long on any one question; if you cannot answer it, carry on to the next question and go back to it later. This will help you to not get stuck on a question and waste your time.

» **READING CHALLENGE 3: 'None of the multiple-choice answer options "feel" right.'**

SOLUTION: Make sure you understand the question types in each part of the paper and the skills you need to answer them. The same question types appear in every Reading and Writing paper. If you know what each part of the paper tests, you will be able to answer the questions with more confidence.

SOLUTION: Decide which answer options are clearly incorrect. If you have to choose between only two options, and not three, you have a greater chance of being right.

SOLUTION: If you find that you are spending too much time on one question and you are not sure of the answer, move on to the next question or the next part. If you have time, you can return to it later. Some people find it easier to answer difficult questions once they have had time to think about them.

» **READING CHALLENGE 4: 'I find it hard to decide what the missing word is in Part 5.'**

SOLUTION: In Reading Part 5 some gaps need a 'grammar' word. These are words such as determiners (e.g. *a, the, much, many*), prepositions (e.g. *on, at, in*) and conjunctions (e.g. *and, but, because*). Make a list of all the types of grammar words you find in practice tests and make sure you understand how they are used.

SOLUTION: Some gaps need words that are part of an expression. For example, a text might need the expression *spend time*, and the word *spend* is missing. Focus on the words around a gap and decide if the missing word is part of an expression. Learn expressions and phrases, not just single words.

Writing

» **WRITING CHALLENGE 1: 'I'm not sure how much time to spend on each question.'**

SOLUTION: You will have about 20 minutes for Writing Parts 6–7. On the day of the exam, wear a watch. While you work, keep an eye on the time. You can use this guide while you write.

Part 6: Total time: 10 minutes	
1 minute	Read the instructions and the short text carefully. Think about what kind of text you have to write, and to whom. Then underline the three messages or pieces of information you have to communicate.
7 minutes	Write a draft of your message on rough paper first. Then write your final answer on the answer sheet.
2 minutes	Check your spelling and watch out for mistakes in your grammar. Make sure you have included all three messages or pieces of information.
Part 7: Total time: 10 minutes	
1 minute	Read the instructions carefully. Identify the three main events of the story. Think about the kind of information that is needed.
7 minutes	Write a draft of the story on rough paper before writing the final answer on your answer sheet.
2 minutes	Check your spelling and watch out for mistakes in your grammar. Make sure you have included information about all three pictures.

SOLUTION: Practise writing within a time limit before the real exam. Start by giving yourself 15 minutes more than the time limit in the exam and slowly cut this down until you can finish writing a few minutes early. You will need this time to read through your work to check for mistakes.

» **WRITING CHALLENGE 2: 'I'm not sure how to improve my vocabulary for the exam.'**

SOLUTION: The Part 6 question might ask you to thank someone, to suggest something or to apologise about something. Make sure you record useful words and phrases to do these things. In the table below there are some examples. Add new ones as you learn them.

Function	Expressions
Thanking	*Many thanks for ...* *Thanks very much for ...*
Suggesting	*Why don't you ...?* *What about ...?* *Try ...* *It would be a good idea to ...*
Apologising	*I'm sorry but ...* *Apologies but ...*

» **WRITING CHALLENGE 3: 'I don't know how to write good notes or emails.'**

SOLUTION: It is easy to begin and end an informal note or email. You can usually begin with *Dear ...* or *Hi/Hello ....* You can usually end with *Write soon* or *See you soon*. But the most important thing is to communicate the three messages or pieces of information.

SOLUTION: In Parts 6 and 7, you should write the correct number of words. For Part 6 do not write fewer than 25 words and don't write more than 35. For Part 7 do not write fewer than 35 words and don't write more than 45 words. This way you won't include points that are irrelevant. Count the words when you finish writing and read your message carefully. Write a draft of your answer on rough paper first before writing your final answer on the answer sheet. Check your spelling, punctuation and grammar.

» **WRITING CHALLENGE 4: 'I don't know how to write a good story for Part 7.'**

SOLUTION: You have to be able to use past tenses well when writing a story, particularly the past simple and past continuous. Practise using these tenses by keeping a diary. Every evening write what happened during the day. For example: *I woke up this morning at about 7.00. I got out of bed and* *went into the bathroom. While I was having a shower, I heard the phone ring.* Keep it simple. Focus on making sure the verb forms are correct and using the two tenses correctly.

SOLUTION: You will get extra marks if you show you can use adjectives and adverbs correctly. Remember: an adjective is used to describe a noun. An adverb gives information about a verb. For example: *There was a loud knock at the door and I got up quickly to see who it was.* Be careful: if you use too many adjectives and adverbs, your writing will seem unnatural.

» **WRITING CHALLENGE 5: 'I'm not good at spelling.'**

SOLUTION: Learn as many words in the *Cambridge English: Key Vocabulary List* on the Cambridge Assessment English website as you can, and revise the spelling as often as possible. Use a good dictionary to look up new words.

SOLUTION: Practise your spelling by testing yourself or by asking a friend or a family member to test you. Make a list of your common spelling mistakes and always check your writing for these.

» **WRITING CHALLENGE 6: 'I don't have good handwriting.'**

SOLUTION: Make sure your handwriting is easy to read. It does not matter if you use capital letters all the time and you do not have to join the letters together within words. But you should be confident that other people can understand your handwriting. Ask a friend to read some of your work and then tell you if it is clear or if any letters or words are difficult to read.

Listening

» **LISTENING CHALLENGE 1: 'I don't know a lot of the words that I hear in the audio recordings or see in the questions.'**

SOLUTION: The instructions for the Listening test are always the same. If you do the practice tests in this book, you will know what you have to do in the real exam. You will also hear each recording twice so if there is a word you do not understand the first time, listen for it the second time.

SOLUTION: After the instructions for Parts 2, 3 and 5 there will be a pause to give you the chance to read the questions. This is very useful. By reading the questions first, you will get an idea about what the people will say, and you can even guess what the answers might be. You will also have time to find the key words before you listen. Then when you listen, you will be able to listen for the right answers.

SOLUTION: Build your vocabulary. Start by downloading the *Cambridge English: Key English Test Vocabulary List* from the Cambridge Assessment English website. This is a list of words that you should understand. Look through the list and make a note of the words you do not know. Then look up their meaning in a dictionary. Knowing these words will help you to do better in the test.

» **LISTENING CHALLENGE 2: 'I don't always understand the speakers because they talk too fast.**

SOLUTION: Listen as much as possible to native English speakers. The more you listen, the better you will understand the English used in the test. Try the following:

• Watch TV programmes or films. The programmes do not have to be educational – comedies and dramas have good examples of natural spoken English. If you find this difficult, watch English-language films with subtitles. Listening can be easier when you can read to check understanding.

• Join an English-language club. Your local library or community centre might have one. If you join one, you will be able to practise speaking English and have the chance to hear native speakers.

• Join an online language community. There may be native speakers of English who want to learn your language and will be happy to practise talking to you using online tools like Skype.

SOLUTION: Download English-language podcasts or radio programmes that you can store on your computer. At first, practise listening for only a minute or two at a time. As you get better, listen for longer. Listen as many times as you need to until you understand the main ideas.

» **LISTENING CHALLENGE 3: 'I find it difficult to do the matching task in Part 5.'**

SOLUTION: You will hear the information in the same order as the things in the first list. Do not choose an option just because you hear a word that you can see in the second list. The speakers often mention the things in the second list but give the correct answer a little later.

» **LISTENING CHALLENGE 4: 'In Part 3, none of the options "feel" right. Sometimes more than one option seems to be correct.'**

SOLUTION: Correct answer options say the same thing as the audio recording but they often use different words, in other words, they paraphrase the recording. Here is an example:

You hear this:	*My house is near the museum.*
The question:	*Where is her house?*
Incorrect answer option:	*Her house is opposite the museum.*
Correct answer option:	*Her house is close to the museum.*

Learn to recognise paraphrasing.

SOLUTION: Decide which answer options are clearly incorrect. Usually, you can ignore an option that has:

- information that is the opposite of the facts in the recording.
- information that does not answer the question.

SOLUTION: Do not spend too much time answering any one question. If you are not sure about an answer, choose the option you like best and move on to the next question. If you spend too long worrying about the correct answer, you might not hear the answer to the next question. You will not lose marks for choosing an incorrect answer.

Speaking

» **SPEAKING CHALLENGE 1: 'I'm not sure how much I have to say when I answer the examiner's questions in Part 1.'**

SOLUTION: This part is just a simple conversation between you and the examiner. It is a chance for them to learn something about you. You do not have to give very long answers but you should say more than 'Yes' or 'No'.

SOLUTION: When you answer Part 1 questions, give a reason for your answer or an example. If the examiner asks *Do you enjoy studying English?* say why you do or do not enjoy it. For example: *Yes, I do, because I like listening to English music and I have English friends who don't speak my language.*

If the examiner says *Tell me about your family*, do not just reply *I have a brother*. When you hear the words *Tell me …* you should answer using at least three sentences. For example: *I have a brother. His name is Pablo and he's two years younger than me. My dad is 42 years old and he's a mechanic. My mum is 40 and she's a teacher.*

» **SPEAKING CHALLENGE 2: 'I'm not very good at asking and answering the questions in Part 2.'**

SOLUTION: Practise making *Yes/No* questions and *Wh-* questions (questions with question words) as much as possible. Write down the questions first and ask a teacher or friend to correct them. Then practise making questions without writing them down. If you make a mistake, repeat the question until you say it correctly.

SOLUTION: Make sure you know the meaning of common question words (e.g. Who? What? Where? When? Why? Which? How? How much? How many? How long?) and practise their pronunciation. Write questions for each question word and use different tenses. Pay special attention to tenses that are often needed in Part 2: the present simple, present continuous, *will* and *going to*. Questions with *can*, *should*, *must* and *have to* are also common.

SOLUTION: Listen to the other candidate's questions carefully and answer using a full sentence. Remember to use the same tense as the question. For example:

Question: *How much does a child's ticket cost?*

Answer: *A child's ticket costs five pounds.*

» **SPEAKING CHALLENGE 3: 'I'm worried that the other candidate will speak better English than me.**

SOLUTION: Do not worry about this and just do your best. The examiners will mark you and the other candidate separately. Prepare for the Speaking paper by practising with friends who speak good English.

SOLUTION: Think carefully before you answer a question. If you do not understand a question, ask the examiner or the other candidate to repeat it. You can do this in a number of ways. For example: *Could you repeat the question, please?* or *I'm sorry. I didn't hear/understand your question. Please repeat it.*

» **SPEAKING CHALLENGE 4: 'I'm worried that the examiners won't understand me. My pronunciation is bad.'**

SOLUTION: At the beginning of Part 1, the examiner will ask you questions using everyday simple English. Some students might feel nervous at the beginning of the Speaking test so these questions will hopefully help you to relax a little. Breathing slowly and not feeling nervous will hopefully help you to speak clearly.

SOLUTION: Having an accent is not a problem. The important thing is to speak clearly so that people can understand you. Ask your friends to listen to a recording of you speaking English. Ask them if it is easy to understand what you are saying. What words do they have difficulty understanding? Practise saying the words you have the most trouble with.

SOLUTION: Some speakers have trouble with certain sounds. For example, some speakers sometimes add e to English words beginning with s, e.g. 'eschool'. Other speakers pronounce the letter w as a v. Find out if speakers from your country have a particular ways of speaking English and practise that area.

SOLUTION: Listen to as much English as possible. When you listen to native English speakers, focus on their pronunciation. You could also listen to English-language radio programmes while you work or watch English-language television in your free time. Start copying the pronunciation you hear to sound more like a native speaker.

SOLUTION: Practise speaking English with native English speakers. To find native English speakers in your area, try going to tourist attractions in your city. You could also join an English-language club at the local library or community centre. Or you could find someone online to practise with.

SOLUTION: If you want people to understand you when you speak, you have to stress words correctly. If you stress the wrong syllable, people might not understand you. For example, in the nouns below, the underlined syllable is stressed:

* celeb<u>ra</u>tion
* ad<u>ve</u>rtisement
* phot<u>og</u>raphy

In the verbs below, a different syllable is stressed:

* <u>ce</u>lebrate
* <u>a</u>dvertise
* <u>ph</u>otograph

Knowing how to pronounce words with more than one syllable is important and you should use a good dictionary to check the stress of any new words.

» **SPEAKING CHALLENGE 5: 'I don't know what to do if I make a mistake and if I should correct myself.'**

SOLUTION: Correcting yourself when you make a mistake is a good way of showing the examiner that you do know the correct word or item of grammar.

SOLUTION: Practise speaking English as much as you can before the exam. One way to do this is to speak to yourself when you are alone. The advantage is that you will be relaxed so you will be less worried about making mistakes. Talk about what has happened during the day, what your plans are for the rest of the week or your opinion of anything that is in the news.

Test 1

TEST 1 READING AND WRITING

Part 1

Questions 1–6

For each question, choose the correct answer.

1

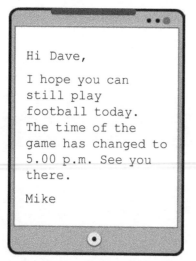

Hi Dave,

I hope you can still play football today. The time of the game has changed to 5.00 p.m. See you there.

Mike

A Dave and Mike will go to the game together.

B Mike thinks Dave wants to change the time of the game.

C Mike wants Dave to know the time of the game.

2

WANTED: Cleaner

No experience needed
Must be hard worker
Phone: 07654 321111

A Somebody wants a cleaner with no experience.

B Somebody wants a cleaner and experience is not important.

C Somebody wants a hard-working cleaner with no experience.

3

To: Diana
From: Ruth

Diana,

Sorry, I will be late for our meeting today. Please start the meeting without me and I will join you when I can.

Ruth

A Ruth will come to the meeting after it starts.

B Ruth wants Diana to wait for her before the meeting.

C Ruth will start the meeting later than she planned to start it.

4

> **Special Supermarket Offer!**
> Today only!
> 5 bananas for £2
> Offer ends at 5 p.m.

A   After 5 p.m. bananas will be more expensive.

B   You can only buy bananas today.

C   Before 5 p.m. there is no special offer.

5

> Henry,
>
> I forgot eggs. We don't need many, but I want you to bake a cake. Can you get some on your way home?
>
> Monika

A   Monika wants to bake a cake.

B   Monika wants Henry to buy eggs.

C   Monika doesn't need eggs.

6

> **LATE NIGHT SHOPPING!**
> Until 8 p.m. in the week and until 10 p.m. at the weekend

A   On Mondays you can shop at 9 p.m.

B   On Fridays you can only shop after 8 p.m.

C   On Saturdays and Sundays you can shop at 9 p.m.

Part 2

Questions 7–13

For each question, choose the correct answer.

		Alan	Rod	Ben
7	Who doesn't have a favourite sport?	A	B	C
8	Who was very good at a sport that was not their favourite?	A	B	C
9	Who had extra lessons in a sport?	A	B	C
10	Who says their body size helps them do a sport?	A	B	C
11	Who has enjoyed football all their life?	A	B	C
12	Who likes to play with a group of other people?	A	B	C
13	Who says they are good at only one sport?	A	B	C

Talking about Sport

Alan

I started playing tennis when I was five years old, but I was never very good at it. My parents really wanted me to do well and paid for me to have lessons outside school, but I always preferred football. I'm good enough to be in a top local team. With tennis, I could never hit the ball where I wanted it to go – it was always too high or too far. Finally, my parents let me stop going to tennis lessons and I've spent my time playing football since then.

Rod

My favourite sport has always been rugby. I've tried other sports and I was good at tennis. I won a tennis competition at school and my sports teacher told me that I was an excellent tennis player. But I didn't enjoy it as much as rugby because I like being part of a team. So I stopped playing tennis when I was about thirteen. My teacher and parents thought I should continue with it, but I preferred rugby.

Ben

I've always played a lot of sport. It's an important part of my life, and since I left school I do a wide variety of different types of sports – golf, rugby, tennis and football. I'm quite good at all of them, but I can't really say that I enjoy one of them more than the others. I'm probably best at rugby because I'm a big person, and it is hard to stop me when I'm running fast.

Part 3

Questions 14–18

For each question, choose the correct answer.

A very clever family

The Smiths are possibly the cleverest family in the country, and now the youngest member, ten-year-old Charlotte, has won a national spelling competition to add to the family's successes. Charlotte is the youngest ever winner of the *National Young Spelling Bee Competition* – the youngest winner before her was her older sister, Helen, who won it when she was eleven.

Charlotte and Helen's older brother, Mark, is also very clever. He finished school early and went to university at the age of fifteen, three years before most young people start their university studies. The children's parents, Charles and Vivien, are both teachers and say their children's success comes from working hard, playing hard and following strict rules about homework and bedtimes.

'Other people think that Charles and I don't let the children have any time to relax and play, and that we're always making them do their homework. But it's not true!' says Vivien. 'We have lots of fun time in the family. But there's a time for fun and there's a time for work, and we make sure the children understand that work comes before play.'

When Charlotte took part in the spelling competition the whole family, including her grandparents, went to watch her. Helen took off a day from school – the first day in her life that she missed going to school. 'I felt bad about missing school,' Helen said, 'but I think it was important to Charlotte that I was there.'

14 Charlotte won the spelling competition

    A after her sister.

    B when she was eleven.

    C when she was older than Helen.

15 Most people

    A go to university early.

    B are like Mark when they go to university.

    C start university at the age of eighteen.

16 Charles and Vivien help their children by

    A letting them relax and play any time they want.

    B making them do their homework before they relax.

    C not letting them have any time to relax and play.

17 When Charlotte won the competition,

    A Helen missed it because she was at school.

    B all the family were there, but not her grandparents.

    C her brother, sister, parents and grandparents were watching.

18 Helen said that

    A Charlotte wanted her to be at the competition.

    B Charlotte missed school for the competition.

    C Charlotte thought competitions were more important than school.

Part 4

Questions 19–24

For each question, choose the correct answer.

The History of Cars

Cars have a long and interesting history. It is difficult to **(19)** ....
when the first car was made. Most people **(20)** .... that it was
made by Karl Benz in 1885. Then in the early twentieth century, cars
(21) .... widely available.

One of the first cars that it was **(22)** .... for ordinary working
people to buy was the Model T Ford, made by Henry Ford in the USA.
Henry Ford found a way of making a large number of cars quickly
and cheaply, and this changed the way that people thought about
how to manufacture things. By 1927, Ford had **(23)** ....
15 million cars.

Today, car-making **(24)** .... jobs to millions of workers. But the
world is changing, and the future of cars is far from clear.

19	**A** say	**B** talk	**C** believe
20	**A** allow	**B** agree	**C** arrive
21	**A** turned	**B** started	**C** became
22	**A** possible	**B** general	**C** ready
23	**A** sold	**B** spent	**C** shown
24	**A** has	**B** wins	**C** gives

Part 5

Questions 25–30

For each question, choose the correct answer.
Write **one** word for each gap.

Example: | **0** | *a* |

> **EMAIL**
>
> From: Helen
>
> To: Henry
>
> Hi Henry,
>
> I hope you're well. I'm having **(0)** .... birthday
> party next week and I hope **(25)** .... can come.
> It's **(26)** .... Friday evening from 8.00 p.m. until
> late. I'm having it **(27)** .... home to keep things
> simple. I'm asking everyone **(28)** .... bring
> some food to share. Can you bring something too?
> If so, **(29)** .... me know what you will bring.
> Then I can tell the others to bring **(30)** ....
> different.
>
> See you soon,
> Helen

Part 6

Questions 31

You want to meet your English friend, Jane, for lunch this weekend.
Write an email to Jane.

In your email:

- suggest meeting for lunch this weekend
- say when you would like to have lunch
- say where you would like to have lunch.

Write **25 words** or more.

Write the email on your answer sheet.

Part 7

Questions 32

Look at the three pictures.
Write the story shown in the pictures.
Write **35 words** or more.

27

Write the story on your answer sheet.

TEST 1 LISTENING

Part 1

Questions 1–5

For each question, choose the correct answer.

---

1 How will David travel?

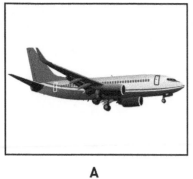

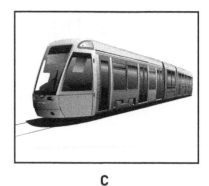

| A | B | C |

2 What time will Roger see the dentist?

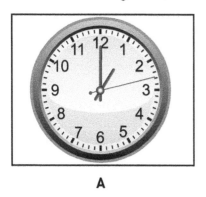

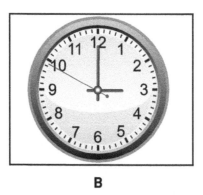

| A | B | C |

3 How much will Vera pay for her lunch?

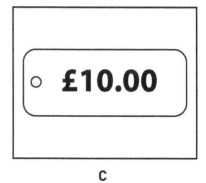

| A | B | C |

4   What will the friends do in the afternoon?

A   B   C

5   What pet will Janet have?

  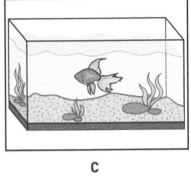

A   B   C

Part 2

02

Questions 6–10

For each question, write the correct answer in the gap. **Write one word or a number or a date or a time.**

You will hear a woman talking to a group of students about the library.

Library Information for Students

Hours during term time:	24 hours a day
Hours outside term time:	**(6)** .... a.m. – 7.00 p.m.
Number of books you can take out:	**(7)** ....
Cost of returning CDs and magazines late:	**(8)** £............... per day
Cost of first library card:	**(9)** ....
To get a card, give in a form and:	**(10)** ....

Part 3

Questions 11–15

For each question, choose the correct answer.

You will hear Jane talking to her friend, David, about going to the cinema.

11 What does Jane want to see at the cinema?

   A She doesn't have a clear idea.

   B She wants to see the new James Bond film.

   C She wants to see a love story.

12 Robert

   A can't come to the cinema.

   B likes action films.

   C prefers not to see the James Bond film.

13 The sad film

   A is about two people who die.

   B doesn't sound good to David.

   C is the only choice.

14 David thinks

   A the comedy would be good for children.

   B the comedy is a good choice for everyone.

   C not everyone likes comedies.

15 Jane

   A will meet David at the cinema at about eight.

   B says the film starts at about eight.

   C will go to David's house at about eight.

Part 4

Questions 16–20

04

For each question, choose the correct answer.

---

16 You will hear a woman talking to her friend about a meal at a restaurant.
What did she eat?

   A steak

   B fish

   C pasta

17 You will hear a man explaining why he was late for work.
Why was he late?

   A He woke up late.

   B The train was late.

   C The bus was slow.

18 You will hear two friends talking about holidays.
Where did Anita go?

   A New York

   B Florida

   C Los Angeles

19 You will hear two friends talking about shopping.
What do they need from the supermarket?

   A potatoes

   B carrots

   C onions

20 You will hear a man talking on the phone.
Why can't he come to the party?

   A He has to go to work early.

   B His mother is visiting him.

   C His mother had an accident.

Part 5

05

Questions 21–25

For each question, choose the correct answer.

You will hear Greta talking to Anthony about holidays.
What type of holiday will each person go on?

Example: Anthony   **B**

People		Type of holiday
21 Julie ☐		**A** sightseeing
22 Greta ☐		**B** walking
23 John ☐		**C** cycling
24 Jenny ☐		**D** camping
25 Ed ☐		**E** no holiday
		F sailing
		G skiing
		H beach

You now have six minutes to write your answers on the answer sheet.

Test 1 SPEAKING

You are Candidate B. Answer the questions.

06–07

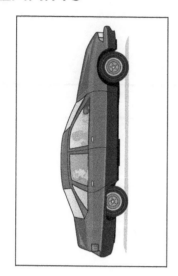

Do you like these different ways of travelling?

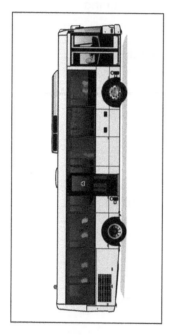

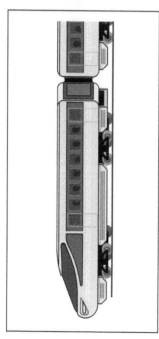

Audio scripts and Model answers on pages 167–223.

Test 2

TEST 2 READING AND WRITING

Part 1

Questions 1–6

For each question, choose the correct answer.

1

Joe, I phoned the ticket office and booked tickets for the play on Saturday. Could you get them on your way home from work tonight?

A Joe will get the tickets at the ticket office on Saturday.

B Joe can book tickets for the play on Saturday.

C Joe can get the tickets before the play on Saturday.

2

Staff must have their identity cards with them at all times in the building.

A Staff mustn't go into the building without their cards.

B Staff don't need their cards when they are in the building.

C Staff need to have their cards in some places in the building.

3

Wednesday's dance class will take place in Studio 5 this week, not 2.

A The time of the dance class has changed

B The place of the dance class has changed.

C The day of the dance class has changed.

4

I'll be late home today. Please prepare dinner. The chicken and potatoes are in the fridge. They must go in the oven for 40 minutes.

What does the person need to do?

A put the food in the oven after 40 minutes

B choose what food from the fridge to eat for dinner

C cook the evening meal in the oven

5

Subject: Office kitchen

Please label all food boxes in the fridge with your name.

Don't leave anything in the fridge for more than a week.

A People can't leave their food in the fridge for a long time.

B People can keep food in the fridge for more than a week.

C People must write what is in their food boxes.

6

**Is your appointment more than 15 minutes late?
Please inform staff at the desk.**

A You must wait for 15 minutes to get an appointment.

B You shouldn't wait for more than 15 minutes.

C You should ask the staff for a 15-minute appointment.

Part 2

Questions 7–13

For each question, choose the correct answer.

		Nikos	Rami	Marcus
7	Who says a place is good if you like outdoor sports?	A	B	C
8	Who says there are things to do at night time?	A	B	C
9	Who says a place is not for people who like swimming?	A	B	C
10	Who likes a place because it is rarely cold there?	A	B	C
11	Who doesn't have a home in the countryside?	A	B	C
12	Who says a place isn't noisy?	A	B	C
13	Who lives near a number of other villages?	A	B	C

Homestay holidays

Nikos

Homestay holidays are becoming very popular, and people everywhere are offering their homes as hotels. My home is in a village in northwest Greece, but it is not for people who enjoy beach holidays. The village is in the mountains and there are 45 other villages in the area. If you are fit, you can walk from one village to the other. The mountain views are fantastic, and you cross old bridges and go past forests where bears live.

Rami

Our home is near the centre of Sydney, Australia's largest city. It is perfect for a homestay holiday. Sydney is a friendly place, with lots of cafés, restaurants and clubs, which are open until long after midnight and where people can enjoy themselves. However, it is noisy at night and there is a lot of traffic during the day. The best thing about Sydney is the weather. It is good all year; it rains in the winter, but it is too warm to snow.

Marcus

Our house is by the sea in the southwest of England, a 15-minute drive from the village of Porthcurno. It is a great place for a relaxing homestay holiday. There are lots of beaches and rivers, and it is very quiet. You can spend a lot of time reading and going for walks. There is a special open-air theatre nearby, on the side of the cliffs. As you watch a show, you can look out to sea. Our area is also great if you enjoy surfing, kayaking and mountain biking.

Part 3

Questions 14–18

For each question, choose the correct answer.

Light pollution: One city turns off its lights

On the evening of 26 September 2019, the streets of Geneva in Switzerland went dark. This usually happens when there is a problem with the electricity, but this time the lights were turned off to allow people to go outside and look at the stars. This is often impossible in a city because of light pollution.

Light pollution is when light from streetlamps or buildings makes the night less dark. There are many reasons why this is a problem. Animals sleep less because they think it is still daytime. Birds that fly to warmer countries in the autumn need to see the moon and stars to find their way, but light pollution makes this difficult. Insects and birds in cities often fly towards lights at night, crash into buildings and die.

Light pollution is also bad for us. It can stop us sleeping and give us headaches. Also, we don't see the same sky that people in the past did. This means we almost never see one of the greatest sights in the world: the millions of stars in our galaxy, the Milky Way. Hundreds of thousands of people have never seen it in their lives.

However, it is not difficult to do a few things to reduce light pollution: we can all turn lights off when we don't need them and we can cover our windows with curtains. If there is less light pollution, we will once again be able to enjoy the beauty of the night sky.

14 The lights were switched off in Geneva on 26 September

    A because there was no electricity in the city.

    B so that people could go out of their houses.

    C to make it easier for people to see the stars.

15 Light pollution is a problem

    A when the night is too dark.

    B when it isn't light enough at night.

    C when there is too much light at night.

16 Light pollutions is bad for some birds because

    A they get lost more easily.

    B they never sleep.

    C they can't see so they crash into buildings.

17 The writer of the article thinks that

    A people today should learn more about the past.

    B it is a pity that people today can't enjoy the night sky.

    C a hundred thousand people have never seen the stars.

18 The writer says that

    A there aren't many things we can do to stop light pollution.

    B it is easy to do something to improve the situation.

    C we can enjoy looking at the stars if we cover our windows.

Part 4

Questions 19–24

For each question, choose the correct answer.

A Favourite Children's Book

Today most people **(19)** .... Lewis Carroll as the author of two books: *Alice's Adventures in Wonderland* and *Through the Looking-Glass*. In the second book, Alice falls asleep one evening. In her dream, she goes **(20)** .... a mirror to the world on the other side. She **(21)** .... out that the countryside there is a giant board in a game of chess, and she must move across it to become a queen. She **(22)** .... people and animals from the first book and some new ones. A few are frightening, but others are **(23)** .... to her. The story ends when Alice becomes a queen and finally **(24)** .... back home.

---

19   **A** return   **B** repeat   **C** remember

20   **A** through   **B** along   **C** away

21   **A** looks   **B** finds   **C** learns

22   **A** knows   **B** meets   **C** speaks

23   **A** kind   **B** careful   **C** real

24   **A** looks up   **B** gets up   **C** wakes up

Part 5

Questions 25–30

For each question, write the correct answer.
Write **one** word for each gap.

Example: | 0 | *my* |

> **EMAIL**
>
> From: Aaron
>
> To: David
>
> David, I've passed **(0)** .... driving test! I took the
> test **(25)** .... morning. I was so worried. Luckily,
> everything went well. I stayed calm **(26)** ....
> followed all the examiner's instructions. She
> **(27)** .... really friendly and helpful. I had difficulty
> parking the car, but in the end I did it. As soon as the
> test finished, the examiner **(28)** .... me I passed.
> Now I have to fill in **(29)** .... form and get my
> licence. Then I will be able to drive **(30)** .... college!
>
> See you on Monday.

Part 6

Questions 31

You want to go cycling on Saturday with your English friend, Paul.
Write an email to Paul.

In your email:

- ask Paul to go cycling with you on Saturday
- say where you want to go cycling
- say where you will meet.

Write **25 words** or more.

Write the email on your answer sheet.

Part 7

Questions 32

Look at the three pictures.
Write the story shown in the pictures.
Write **35 words** or more.

Write the story on your answer sheet.

TEST 2 LISTENING

Part 1

08

Questions 1–5

For each question, choose the correct answer.

---

1   What might Mark look like now?

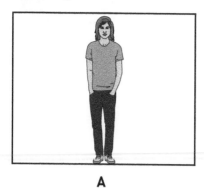
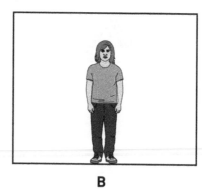
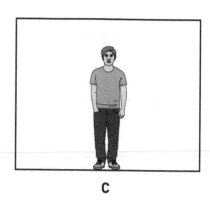

A   B   C

2   What will the woman probably study next year?

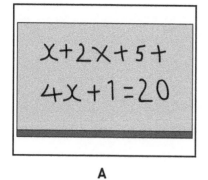

A   B   C

3 What is David making for dinner?

A   B   C

4 What time does the exam begin?

A   B   C

5 Where does the woman think she lost her purse?

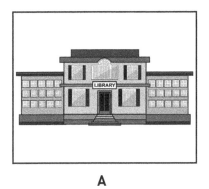 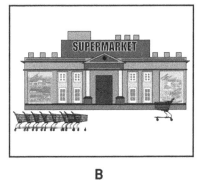 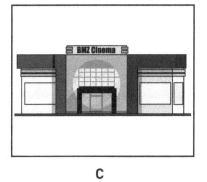

A   B   C

Part 2

09

Questions 6–10

For each question, write the correct answer in the gap. **Write one word or a number or a date or a time.**

You will hear a woman talking about her work experience.

Work experience: Jessica Chapman

Job: Online language teacher

Taught: Students in **(6)** ....

Lessons: **(7)** .... hours a week

Number of students: three to **(8)** ....

In lessons: talked, played **(9)** .... and sang
                                        songs

Worked: from **(10)** .... to September

Part 3

Questions 11–15

For each question, choose the correct answer.

You will hear Laura talking to her friend John about her trip to Scotland.

11 Which city didn't Laura visit?

    A Aberdeen

    B Glasgow

    C Dundee

12 How many people went with Laura?

    A two

    B three

    C four

13 They stayed

    A in guest houses

    B in hotels

    C at the universities

14 What does Laura like about St Andrews?

    A She likes the area.

    B A lot of people live there.

    C The buildings there are old.

15 Laura wasn't sure about living in Edinburgh because

    A it is a big city.

    B there isn't enough to do there.

    C it costs a lot of money to live there.

Part 4

Questions 16–20

For each question, choose the correct answer.

---

16 You will hear a teacher talking to a student.
What does he say about her work?

    A Her homework and project were both excellent.

    B Her project was excellent, but her homework was not very good.

    C Her project was good, but her homework was better.

17 You will hear a man talking about to his friend about a photograph.
Who is the woman in the photograph?

    A his sister

    B his cousin

    C his aunt

18 You will hear a man talking to his friend about a jacket.
Why did he buy it?

    A to look good

    B to keep warm

    C to wear to work

19 You will hear a mother talking to her son.
Why is she unhappy?

    A He made the floor dirty.

    B He didn't tell her where he was.

    C He didn't remember to buy milk.

20 You will hear two friends talking about their day.
What did they do first?

    A They went shopping.

    B They had something to eat.

    C They went to a museum.

Part 5

Questions 21–25

For each question, choose the correct answer.

You will hear Sally talking to James about different documents and books. Which person do they belong to?

Example:

Dad   F

People

21   Jane   ☐

22   Mum   ☐

23   Granny   ☐

24   Grandpa   ☐

25   George   ☐

Documents

A   notebook

B   diary

C   postcards

D   menu

E   bills

F   passport

G   photo album

H   driving licence

You now have six minutes to write your answers on the answer sheet.

Test 2 SPEAKING

You are Candidate B. Answer the questions.

13–14

Do you like these different places to live?

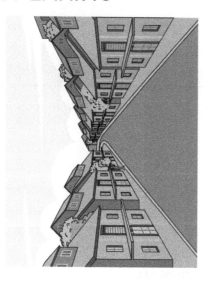

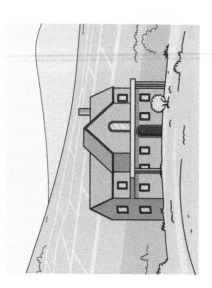

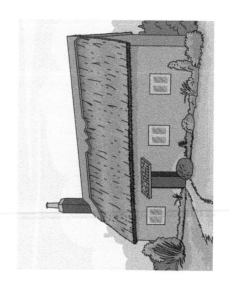

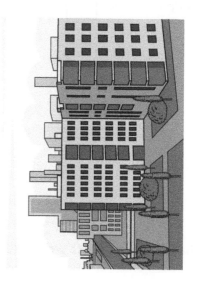

Audio scripts and Model answers on pages 167–223.

Test 3

TEST 3 READING AND WRITING

Part 1

Questions 1–6

For each question, choose the correct answer.

1

Hi Jane,

I'll be home late tonight. Can you cook? Or I can get something on the way home. Fish and chips?

Michael

A Michael wants Jane to cook fish and chips.

B Michael wants to eat fish and chips on the way home.

C Michael offers to buy fish and chips for dinner.

2

High-speed internet offer:
Buy for 12 months and pay half-price!
Offer ends soon.

A You get a special price on six months of internet.

B You get a better price if you buy internet for a year.

C You don't have to decide quickly.

3

Mark,

Sorry I missed you. I had to go out to my mother's house. Can we do it tomorrow? Same time and place?

Hannah

A Hannah wants to meet Mark at her mother's house tomorrow.

B Hannah misses Mark and wants to go to his house.

C Mark went to Hannah's house but she was not at home.

4

STAFF PARKING ONLY
For extra spaces and
student parking, turn left

A This is the only place where staff can park.

B Extra space is only for students.

C Turn left if you are staff and the car park is full.

5

Hello,

Is your bike still
for sale? I'm
interested in it
if it doesn't need
any work and I can
test ride it.

Regards,
Ben

A Ben wants to see if he likes the bike.

B Ben doesn't need the bike for work.

C Ben can test the bike.

6

To: Joseph

From: Briony

Dear Joseph,

I'm unhappy that you were late a second time this week. Please make an appointment with Jenny to speak to me.

Regards,
Briony

A Briony will be unhappy if Joseph is late for a second time this week.

B Briony wants Joseph to explain to her why he was late.

C Joseph must explain why he was late to Jenny.

Part 2

Questions 7–13

For each question, choose the correct answer.

		Gerald	Simone	Frank
7	Who enjoys being alone?	A	B	C
8	Who likes learning about the different ways that people live?	A	B	C
9	Who explores places that you cannot get to by car?	A	B	C
10	Who has to travel with another person?	A	B	C
11	Who thinks a lot about what to take with them?	A	B	C
12	Who spent time away from home when they were young?	A	B	C
13	Who explains why their transport is better than others?	A	B	C

Explorers

Gerald

When I was a boy, my parents worked in Africa for two years. We visited lots of exciting places there and I have loved travelling and exploring since then. I usually choose to travel alone because it is easier to meet people that way. I often stay with the new friends I make on my journeys, and finding out about new cultures is my favourite part of exploring.

Simone

My favourite places are in the cold parts of the world. There are some areas, covered in snow and ice, where almost no one has ever been before. I usually go on foot because there are no roads. I plan my trips very carefully – I like to be well prepared and I take lots of special equipment with me. I sometimes go for days and weeks without seeing other people – I like the opportunity that gives me to think about my life and to make plans.

Frank

I do most of my exploring by boat. It can take me weeks to get somewhere I could drive to in a day, but it is all about the journey. I always take someone else because my boat needs two people and I don't think I would like to go alone. There usually aren't many people at all in the places that I explore, so I don't often meet new people. My boat is quite small so I can get to places that other, bigger boats can't get to. That makes travelling even more interesting.

Part 3

Questions 14–18

For each question, choose the correct answer.

Businessperson of the Year

Henrietta Dawson, a businessperson from Portsmouth, is the new Businessperson of the Year. Henrietta heard she had won the prize at a dinner in London last night.

'I can't believe I won the title!' Henrietta said when she found out. 'There are hundreds of good, hard-working businesspeople out there, so when people tell you that you're the best it's just fantastic.'

Henrietta runs three companies that make food and drink to sell to hotels and restaurants in and around her hometown. 'I couldn't have done it without my parents and husband. They've given me a lot of help,' Henrietta said.

Henrietta's mother was also a successful businessperson and taught her daughter that anything is possible if you work hard. Henrietta is also lucky because her husband, Pete, put his own career on hold to look after their two young children.

Henrietta is the first woman to win the title. Last year's winner, Tom Lawson, who runs a successful tourism company, was at the dinner too. 'The competition is an important way to get people interested in starting their own businesses,' he told the audience. 'Of course, not everyone wants to do it, but you don't need to come from a rich family to be a successful businessperson.'

Henrietta could one day be a rich woman. But she isn't one yet; the money she makes goes back into her businesses, not into her pocket.

14 Henrietta

    A has food and drink companies in Portsmouth.

    B sells hotels and restaurants in her hometown.

    C has companies which sell food and drink in London.

15 Henrietta

    A wasn't surprised when she won the title.

    B was told by many businesspeople that she was the best.

    C didn't know she would win the competition.

16 Henrietta's husband

    A is a lucky man.

    B has helped her become successful.

    C also has a successful career.

17 Tom thinks the competition is important

    A because everyone is interested in starting a business.

    B because it shows that business is not only for some people.

    C because anyone can run a business.

18 Henrietta

    A might be rich in the future.

    B has become a rich woman.

    C uses her money to start new businesses.

Part 4

Questions 19–24

For each question, choose the correct answer.

Florence Nightingale

Florence Nightingale was born in 1820. Her parents gave her an excellent education, but two hundred years ago the daughters of rich parents didn't have careers. Their families expected them to **(19)** .... married and stay at home. But Florence wanted to be a nurse and **(20)** .... sick people. In 1854 she travelled to Turkey. At that time, Britain and some other countries were fighting a war against Russia. Florence worked very **(21)** .... to improve the care of injured soldiers in the hospital. She became **(22)** .... all over the world for her work there.

Florence started a school for nurses in 1860 and, for the first **(23)** .... , being a nurse became a real job. She also understood that it was very important to **(24)** .... things clean in hospitals.

Florence died in 1910 at the age of ninety.

---

19 **A** get   **B** become   **C** have

20 **A** look at   **B** look for   **C** look after

21 **A** certainly   **B** hard   **C** best

22 **A** special   **B** favourite   **C** famous

23 **A** time   **B** age   **C** year

24 **A** let   **B** be   **C** keep

Part 5

Questions 25–30

For each question, write the correct answer.
Write **one** word for each gap.

Example:

0	*you*

> **EMAIL**
>
> From: John
>
> To: Mark
>
> Dear Mark,
>
> I hope **(0)** .... and your family are well. I am visiting London next week and I thought it would be nice **(25)** .... meet. We haven't seen each other **(26)** .... a long time! I am staying in London **(27)** .... Tuesday to Sunday evening. **(28)** .... you like to meet me somewhere for a snack or **(29)** .... meal? I am busy most days with meetings, but I'll be free **(30)** .... the evenings and at the weekend. It would be great to see you again.
>
> Best wishes,
> John

Part 6

Questions 31

You want your English friend, Roger, to buy you some fruit and vegetables from the supermarket. Write a note to Roger.

In your note:

- ask Roger to buy you some fruit and vegetables from the supermarket
- say what fruit and vegetables you want
- say when you will give him the money.

Write **25 words** or more.

Write the note on your answer sheet.

Part 7

Questions 32

Look at the three pictures.
Write the story shown in the pictures.
Write **35 words** or more.

Write the story on your answer sheet.

TEST 3 LISTENING

Part 1

Questions 1–5

For each question, choose the correct answer.

---

1   What time is Margaret's train?

A

B

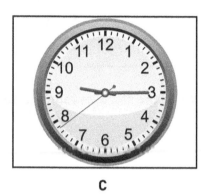

C

2   What will Mary bring to the party?

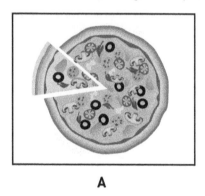

A

B

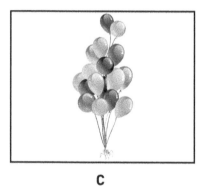

C

3   What will Roberta do this afternoon?

A

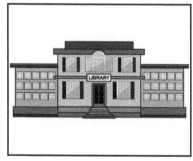

B

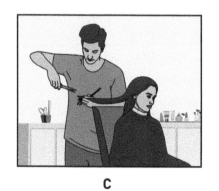

C

4   What will the friends eat for dinner?

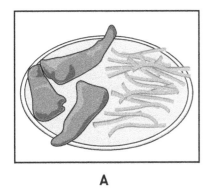
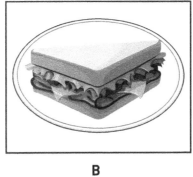
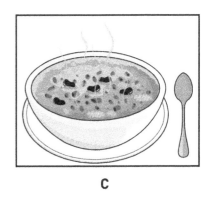

| A | B | C |

5   What job does Kevin's son have?

| A | B | C |

Part 2

16

Questions 6–10

For each question, write the correct answer in the gap. **Write one word or a number or a date or a time.**

You will hear a speaker giving information to students about staying in university flats.

Information about Student Flats

Number of students sharing type 1 flat:	10
Longest term:	**(6)** .... weeks long
Price of type 1 flat for final term:	**(7)** £..............
Number of students sharing type 2 flat:	**(8)** ....
Term 1 dates for flats:	**(9)** .... September–20 December
Monday–Thursday	Students must be **(10)** .... after 10 p.m.

Part 3

17

Questions 11–15

For each question, choose the correct answer.

You will hear Peter talking to his friend Linda about going camping.

11 Who is Peter going camping with?

    A colleagues

    B old school friends

    C colleagues and old school friends

12 How many nights are Peter and his friends going camping for?

    A three nights

    B two nights

    C one night

13 Peter

    A thinks his house is dirty.

    B wants a cleaner for his house.

    C needs somebody to paint his bathroom.

14 How many tents are they taking?

    A one

    B two

    C four

15 Peter and his friends

    A will have simple breakfasts in cafes and restaurants.

    B will have their own milk and cereal for breakfast.

    C will pay for three meals a day.

Part 4

18

Questions 16–20

For each question, choose the correct answer.

---

16 You will hear a woman shopping for shoes.
Which pair of shoes does she buy?

A the brown ones

B the green ones

C the black ones

17 You will hear a woman describing something she lost.
What did she lose?

A a suitcase

B a purse

C a handbag

18 You will hear two friends talking.
What is Paul going to make?

A a cake

B an omelette

C fried eggs

19 You will hear a man talking about his holiday to his friend.
What animal did he ride?

A an elephant

B a camel

C a horse

20 You will hear a woman talking to her friend.
Why is she upset?

A Jean was not at home.

B The taxi was expensive.

C The taxi driver didn't help with her luggage.

Part 5

Questions 21–25

For each question, choose the correct answer.

You will hear John and Fiona talking about what to do with the family at the activity centre. What activity will each person do?

Example:

John   B

People		Activity
21 Billy	☐	**A** tennis
22 Fred	☐	**B** golf
23 Fiona	☐	**C** football
24 Keith	☐	**D** swimming
25 Shona	☐	**E** horse riding
		F table tennis
		G badminton
		H no activity

You now have six minutes to write your answers on the answer sheet.

Test 3 SPEAKING

You are Candidate B. Answer the questions.

20–21

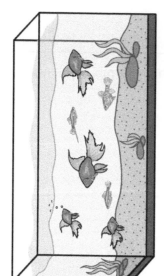

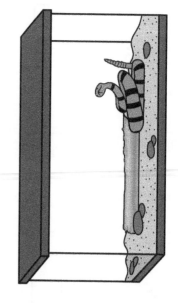

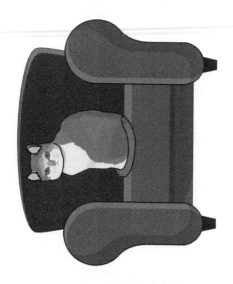

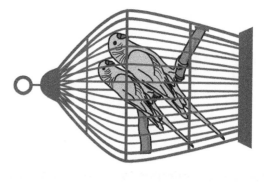

Do you like these different pets?

Audio scripts and Model answers on pages 167–223.

Test 4

TEST 4 READING AND WRITING

Part 1

Questions 1–6

For each question, choose the correct answer.

1

From: Sofia

To: David

Hi from Oslo!
I'm having such
fun skiing in the
mountains. Here
are some photos
I took.

See you on
Saturday!

A Sofia is writing to tell David when she will see him.

B Sofia is writing to send David some pictures.

C Sofia is writing to tell David where she is going on holiday.

2

To: Paula

From: Ian

Call me this evening after your biology class. My mobile phone isn't working, so here's my landline: 067123456.

A Ian wants Paula to call him at home.

B Ian wants Paula to call him on his mobile.

C Ian wants Paula to call him after his biology class.

3

Customers can apply to become gym members online.
Please collect ID cards from the gym.

A People can get their gym ID cards online.

B People can apply to become members on the internet.

C People can only apply for membership at the gym.

4

Hi George,

The new technology centre is opening this weekend. I wonder if it will have cool things. Let me know before Friday.

Kelly

What does George need to do?

A visit the technology centre at the weekend

B tell Kelly if the technology centre is open this weekend

C tell Kelly if he can go to the technology centre this weekend

5

**Sports store
All trainers half price!
New season football kit in!
New sports equipment!**

A You pay less for all clothes at the store.

B You can only buy trainers at the store.

C You can find clothes for different seasons at the store

6

Weekly meeting

Change of day and time: Tuesday, not Monday.

Be there at 9.30 a.m.!

A The meeting is on Monday at 9.30 a.m.

B The meeting doesn't usually start at 9.30 a.m.

C There is a meeting every Tuesday morning.

Part 2

Questions 7–13

For each question, choose the correct answer.

		Paul	Mark	Samuel
7	Who started dancing before he had lessons?	A	B	C
8	Who didn't start dancing because of a family member?	A	B	C
9	Who didn't enjoy dancing at first?	A	B	C
10	Who already has a successful career as a dancer?	A	B	C
11	Who couldn't continue dancing because he had a problem?	A	B	C
12	Who studied two kinds of dance?	A	B	C
13	Who stopped doing a sport when he started dancing?	A	B	C

A love of dancing

Paul

My mum was a professional dancer, and I had my first ballet lesson when I was six. I hated it and never went again. Mum was disappointed, but then she suggested that I should try modern dance. It was a brilliant idea. I loved it. When I left school, I joined a modern dance company. Unfortunately, a few years later I had a bad accident. Now my right leg isn't strong enough for me to dance, but I'm training to be a dance teacher.

Mark

My love for dance began when I was four. My big sister took ballet lessons, and when she practised at home, I watched and copied her. I asked my mum and dad if I could have ballet lessons too. They were surprised, but they agreed. Soon I was better than my sister. I studied ballet and modern dance, and when I left school I was offered a place in a modern dance company. One day I want to be a star and dance in musicals.

Samuel

I became interested in dance when one of my friends started going to modern dance lessons. As a joke, I went to a class with him one day. To my surprise, I enjoyed it and the teacher said I was good. I started going to class three times a week, so I didn't have time for football anymore. Some people at school laughed at me. They aren't laughing now. I am a dancer with a famous dance company. Dance is my life.

Part 3

Questions 14–18

For each question, choose the correct answer.

CopenHill

Most tourists to Copenhagen want to see its famous sights: the statue of the Little Mermaid in the harbour, the Tivoli Gardens, old palaces and museums. The Danish capital is also famous for its beautiful modern buildings, and in 2019 another building was completed in the city: the Amager Resource Centre (ARC), also known as CopenHill. It has many visitors, but it is unusual because it is not a hotel, a bank, an office block, a museum or a shopping centre. It is a waste resource centre. This means that 400,000 tons of rubbish are brought inside the building every year. There, it is burned to heat 150,000 homes and make electricity for 550,000 people.

However, Bjarke Ingels, the architect who designed CopenHill, wanted the 90-metre-high building to do more than burn rubbish. It is the only place in the country where people can go skiing. The roof is like a mountain with a 400-metre ski slope. It is not white, but green: bright green in the middle and dark green at the sides. Ingels chose green because white would get dirty too quickly. Visitors can also go snowboarding, running or walking on CopenHill, and after an enjoyable day of activity they can relax in the café. The outside of the building also has the world's highest climbing wall: 85 metres!

The idea that a building can have many very different uses is exciting, and it will be interesting to see what Copenhagen will offer visitors in the future.

14 Which statement is true?

    A Old buildings in Copenhagen are not as beautiful as modern ones.

    B Tourists prefer Copenhagen's old buildings to its modern ones.

    C Visitors to Copenhagen can enjoy a variety of different sights.

15 CopenHill

    A is in the centre of the city.

    B is near a shopping centre.

    C is a popular place.

16 The ski slope

    A is inside the CopenHill building.

    B is 90 metres in length.

    C is on the roof of the building.

17 The ski slope isn't white because

    A white is difficult to keep clean.

    B green is Ingels' favourite colour.

    C bright green is used in the middle.

18 Visitors to CopenHill

    A can enjoy different activities there in the future.

    B can have something to drink there.

    C can climb the highest building in the city.

Part 4

Questions 19–24

For each question, choose the correct answer.

Stonehenge

Stonehenge is one of the world's most famous monuments. It is a circle of huge stones in the south of England. People started making it 5,000 years ago, but they took over 1,000 years to **(19)** .... it. If you **(20)** .... Stonehenge today, you will see many stones still standing, but it is a mystery how people **(21)** .... them there. The stones are very **(22)** ....: the smaller stones are about 3,600 kilograms each, and the bigger ones are about 22,000 kilograms! Archeologists believe that people carried some stones 32 kilometres, but it is possible that the bigger ones came from 225 kilometres **(23)** .... in Wales. They **(24)** .... that people carried the stones to a river and put them on simple boats. They then took them to the stone circle.

19	**A** grow		**B** build		**C** have
20	**A** return		**B** miss		**C** visit
21	**A** brought		**B** bought		**C** became
22	**A** high		**B** hard		**C** heavy
23	**A** far		**B** away		**C** there
24	**A** think		**B** hope		**C** wish

Part 5

Questions 25–30

For each question, write the correct answer.
Write **one** word for each gap.

Example:

0	*into*

```
EMAIL

From:  Jade

To:    Alex

Sorry I haven't written for such a long time! I've just
moved (0) ............ my new room at university and I only
got my internet connection today. It's good (25) ............
be online again! My room is in (26) ............ large
building and there are lots of other students here. I've
already met a few of (27) ............ . The people here
(28) ............ really friendly.

In my room, there's a bed, a wardrobe for my clothes,
a chair (29) ............ a large desk for my computer. It's
(30) ............ to the window, so I'll have good light when
I'm studying.

I'll write again with more news soon!
```

Part 6

Questions 31

You are going to visit a new library on Wednesday with your English friend, Peter.
Write an email to Peter.

In your email:

- say where you want to meet.
- say what time you want to meet.
- say what books you would like to borrow from the library.

Write **25 words** or more.

Write the email on your answer sheet.

Part 7

Questions 32

Look at the three pictures.
Write the story shown in the pictures.
Write **35 words** or more.

Write the story on your answer sheet.

TEST 4 LISTENING

Part 1

Questions 1–5

For each question, choose the correct answer.

---

1   Who is Jenny's brother?

A

B

C

2   What will they have for dinner?

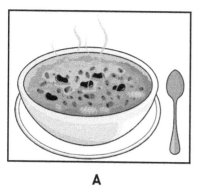

A

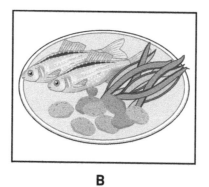

B

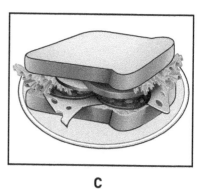

C

3   Where is Carla's tent?

A

B

C

4 What is Louis writing to his friend?

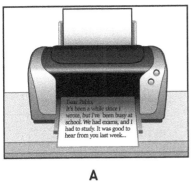

A

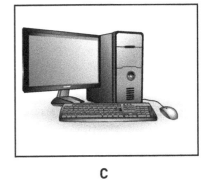

Hi Pablo,
I saw this magazine
and I thought of you.
It's got some good
articles

B

C

5 What did Tom forget to bring to his last exam?

A

B

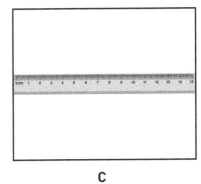

C

Part 2

23

Questions 6–10

For each question, write the correct answer in the gap. **Write one word or a number or a date or a time.**

You will hear a student giving a presentation about Thomas Edison, the famous inventor.

Thomas Alva Edison

Nationality:	American
Date of birth:	11 **(6)** 1847
Moved to New York City:	1869
Made:	**(7)** $............ from his inventions.
1876:	Opened a laboratory in Menlo **(8)** ....
1884:	His first wife, Mary Stilwell, **(9)** ....
1886:	Married his second wife, Mina Miller, and moved to West Orange in New Jersey.
Died:	18 October **(10)** ....

Part 3

24

Questions 11–15

For each question, choose the correct answer.

You will hear Emma talking to her friend Fabio about a fashion show.

11 Who did Fabio go to the fashion show with?

    A He went with some friends.

    B He went with a family member.

    C He went on his own.

12 Which day did Emma go to the fashion show?

    A Friday

    B Saturday

    C Sunday

13 Which show didn't Emma see?

    A the costume show

    B the children's fashion show

    C the sports clothes show

14 Who didn't like the sports clothes show?

    A Fabio and Anna

    B Emma and Anna

    C Fabio, Emma and Melissa

15 What is Emma making for the 'Beautiful Plastic' show?

    A jewellery

    B shoes and a bag

    C clothes

Part 4

Questions 16–20

25

For each question, choose the correct answer.

___

16 You will hear two friends talking about an accident.
What did Matt break?

   A his arm

   B his head

   C his leg

17 You will hear two people talking about some keys.
Where did the man leave them?

   A in the hall

   B in the kitchen

   C in the living room

18 You will hear two friends talking in a restaurant.

What does the woman decide to eat?

   A a cheeseburger

   B a salad

   C a pizza

19 You will hear a man talking a friend about his grandparents.
What are they doing this weekend?

   A They are having a birthday party.

   B They are meeting their new neighbours.

   C They are moving to a new house.

20 You will hear a woman talking to a friend about going to the airport.
How will she get there?

   A by bus

   B by taxi

   C by train

Part 5

26

Questions 21–25

For each question, choose the correct answer.

You will hear Max talking to Ellie about a barbecue.
What will each person bring?

Example:

Ellie | G |

People

21   George   [   ]

22   Jack   [   ]

23   Max   [   ]

24   Sophie   [   ]

25   Oscar   [   ]

Food or drink

A salad

B curry

C fruit

D drinks

E sausages

F ice

G burgers

H desserts

You now have six minutes to write your answers on the answer sheet.

Test 4 SPEAKING

You are Candidate B. Answer the questions.

27–28

Do you like these different types of entertainment?

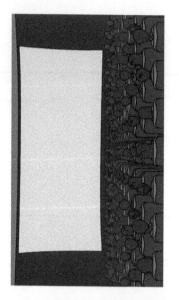

Audio scripts and Model answers on pages 167–223.

Test 5

TEST 5 READING AND WRITING

Part 1

Questions 1–6

For each question, choose the correct answer.

1

Hi Jon,

Sorry to hear you can't make today's meeting. Shall we try for tomorrow? What about after the business lunch at 3.00 p.m.?

Hank

A Hank is inviting Jon to a business lunch.

B Hank is busy today and wants to change the meeting time.

C Hank is suggesting a new time for the meeting.

2

DO NOT ENTER!
Staff and business
visitors only.
No customers past
this sign.

A Nobody can enter here.

B Some people can enter here.

C Customers can go past this sign.

3

To: Janet
From: Tina

Dear Janet,

Michael's sick. Could you take notes at the meeting? I know you're busy, so it's OK to say no.

Regards,
Tina

A Janet is busy and cannot take notes at the meeting.

B Michael is sick and cannot take notes at the meeting.

C Tina thinks Janet can take notes at the meeting.

4

FOR SALE: PIANO
Perfect working order
Beautiful sound
Some small marks
Call: 0777654321

A The piano is nearly as good as new.

B The piano is as beautiful as a new one.

C Someone will deliver the piano if you call this number.

5

Hi Sissie,

Guess what! Cindy's coming back to town! She's arriving at 5 and then we're getting something to eat. Want to join us?

Tracy

A Cindy is coming to town for the first time.

B Tracy and Sissie are getting something to eat at five.

C Tracy is inviting Sissie for a meal.

6

ZOO
Under 14s have to be with an adult. School groups must take guided tour.

A A fourteen-year-old cannot go to the zoo without an adult.

B A school group cannot visit the zoo with a guide.

C A school group can only visit the zoo if they have a tour guide.

Part 2

Questions 7–13

For each question, choose the correct answer.

		Amy	Bao	Nigel
7	Who likes to eat food cooked outside?	A	B	C
8	Whose city is famous for its transport?	A	B	C
9	Who describes a part of their city where you can see old and new things?	A	B	C
10	Whose city is not the most popular in the country for tourists?	A	B	C
11	Who likes to eat dishes from different countries?	A	B	C
12	Who describes more than one way to see the sights in their city?	A	B	C
13	Who likes walking around their city?	A	B	C

My City

Amy

I live in New York and I love it! It has over eight million people who speak 800 different languages. 60 million visitors come here every year. My favourite way to get around is on foot, especially to places such as Times Square, one of the most famous and popular tourist sights. You get the feel of New York here. From there it's only a ten-minute walk to Hell's Kitchen, where you can get delicious food from all over the world.

Bao

I'm from Shanghai, one of the biggest cities in China. 24 million people live here. It's the second most popular city for tourists in China. The Bund is a great place to visit; you can see historical buildings and modern futuristic buildings, and you can enjoy the view if you take a boat tour along the river. I love going to Chenghuanmiao Old Street, where you can eat food prepared on the street. Both local people and visitors love it!

Nigel

I was born in London and I don't think I'll ever leave! It's the economic, shopping, cultural and financial centre of the UK, and millions of tourists come here every year. London is famous for its red buses and tourists love using them to get around. Many companies offer bus tours around the most interesting places to visit. You can also see the city if you take a boat tour through the centre of the city. My favourite place is Soho because there are lots of restaurants and exciting things to do and see there.

Part 3

Questions 14–18

For each question, choose the correct answer.

Star makes Simon's restaurant the best in town

One, two or even three Michelin stars are given to restaurants with exceptionally good food, and chef Simon Jones has just won one for his restaurant, The Tiger. It is the first time that a restaurant in Moreton has got a Michelin star and Simon is delighted. He is very proud of it, and he is having a party for friends, family and customers. 'I'm so pleased with the star,' Simon says. 'It shows how much we have improved in the past ten years since we started the business.'

Michelin stars are not easy to win and Simon hopes it will help his business. The Tiger is a fish and seafood restaurant, which makes the star even more special. The restaurant is over 80 kilometres from the sea, so the fish and seafood have to travel a long way by train every day.

Simon's wife, Angela, has been at the restaurant since its beginning. She and Simon met when she got a job doing the washing-up. Five years ago, she left the kitchen and now she takes bookings and shows customers to their tables.

'It's great news, and not only for us!' Angela says. 'Hopefully, the Michelin star will bring a lot of new visitors into the area. If our business grows, there will be more jobs in the town for local people and they won't have to leave to find work.'

Simon and Angela play an active part in local life, visiting schools to share their business experience and offering work experience to school children.

14 The Tiger

    A is a place where stars like to eat.

    B was the first restaurant in Moreton.

    C is not a new restaurant.

15 It was very difficult for Simon's fish restaurant to win a star

    A because fish and seafood are not easy to cook.

    B because he has to travel long distances.

    C because it is so far from the sea.

16 Angela

    A worked in the kitchen when she started at the restaurant.

    B got a job doing the washing-up five years ago.

    C left the restaurant five years ago.

17 The star for the restaurant is good because

    A more local people will eat at the restaurant.

    B a lot of visitors come to Moreton.

    C it can help the business get bigger.

18 Simon and Angela

    A visit schools so that their business can grow.

    B give opportunities to local children.

    C play with local children.

Part 4

Questions 19–24

For each question, choose the correct answer.

Helen Keller

Helen Keller was born in the USA in 1880. When she was nineteen months old she was very sick and nearly **(19)** .... She got better, but she lost the use of her eyes and ears, so she could not see or **(20)** .... Her **(21)** .... life was very difficult. She couldn't go to school with other children, but her parents **(22)** .... a teacher for her. When she was seven, she finally began learning to **(23)** .... sign language, and her life changed.

Helen studied hard and went to university. This was an amazing achievement for a person like Helen. As an adult, she spent a lot of time talking to people about her life.

Helen became **(24)** .... during her lifetime and there are many books and films about her.

---

19   **A** finished   **B** passed   **C** died

20   **A** hear   **B** listen   **C** watch

21   **A** young   **B** child   **C** early

22   **A** found   **B** looked   **C** caught

23   **A** use   **B** have   **C** be

24   **A** favourite   **B** famous   **C** known

Part 5

Questions 25–30

For each question, write the correct answer.
Write **one** word for each gap.

Example: | 0 | / |

<table>
<tr><td>**EMAIL**</td></tr>
<tr><td>From: Molly</td></tr>
<tr><td>To: Michael</td></tr>
</table>

Dear Michael,

(0) .... am writing to say a big thank you. It was very kind of you and your wife to invite us **(25)** .... your home. You have such **(26)** .... lovely place! It was wonderful to meet your family. Our daughters loved playing football with your children **(27)** .... Saturday afternoon. The meal in **(28)** .... evening was delicious.

I would **(29)** .... to invite you and your family to come and stay with us one weekend soon. We are very busy this month, but what about one weekend **(30)** .... month?

Molly

Part 6

Question 31

You want to invite your English friend, Hannah, to your birthday party.
Write her an email.

In your email:

- invite Hannah to your birthday party
- say when and where it is
- tell her if she should bring anything.

Write **25 words** or more.

Write the email on your answer sheet.

Part 7

Question 32

Look at the three pictures.
Write the story shown in the pictures.
Write **35 words** or more.

Write the story on your answer sheet.

TEST 5 LISTENING

Part 1

Questions 1–5

For each question, choose the correct answer.

---

1 What will they buy Timmy for his birthday?

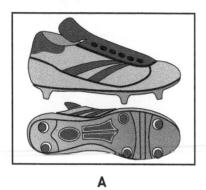

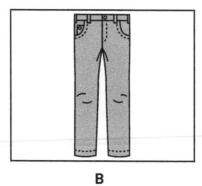

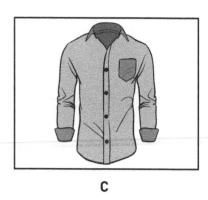

| A | B | C |

2 What time will they meet?

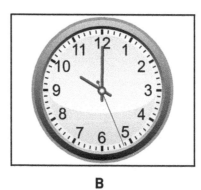

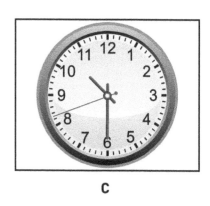

| A | B | C |

3 Where will they go skiing?

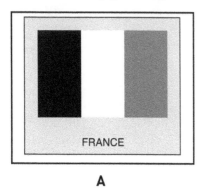

FRANCE

ITALY

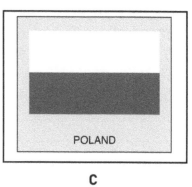

POLAND

| A | B | C |

4   How will the friends travel?

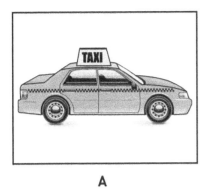

A

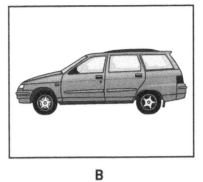

B

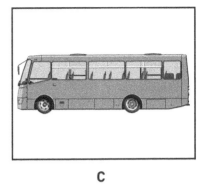

C

5   How much will the woman pay for the bicycle?

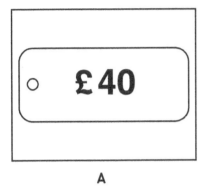

A

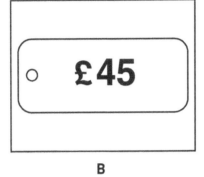

B

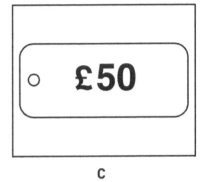

C

Part 2

Questions 6–10

30

For each question, write the correct answer in the gap. **Write one word or a number or a date or a time.**

You will hear a speaker giving information about a skiing trip.

Skiing trip	
Country:	Italy
Dates of trip:	2nd – **(6)** .... January
Cost of trip:	**(7)** £...............
Not included in price:	Lunch and **(8)** ....
Free lessons:	Every **(9)** ....
Lessons are important for:	**(10)** ....

Part 3

31

Questions 11–15

For each question, choose the correct answer.

You will hear Nigel talking to his friend Elizabeth about his course at university.

11 Nigel is happy because

    A he can study with friends.

    B he can spend his spare time with his friends.

    C he can study with his best friends.

12 How many students will be in Nigel's group?

    A two

    B three

    C four

13 What do they have to do in their project?

    A start selling things to students

    B start a student shop

    C start a new business

14 Nigel and Jenny

    A want to sell pens, notebooks and bags to students.

    B want to sell food and drink to students.

    C have different ideas about what to sell.

15 Elizabeth thinks

    A students are good at selling things.

    B students often can't buy things.

    C students like spending money.

Part 4

32

Questions 16–20

For each question, choose the correct answer.

___

16 You will hear a woman talking to a friend about an experience.
Where did she go?

A to a film

B to a play

C to an opera

17 You will hear a man and a woman talking.
Where has the man been?

A fishing

B sailing

C swimming

18 You will hear a man and a woman talking.
What will they have for breakfast?

A cereal, eggs and toast

B eggs and toast

C toast

19 You will hear two friends talking.
What did Karen want to buy?

A clothes

B food

C books

20 You will hear two friends talking.
What new piece of furniture has David got?

A a sofa

B a table

C an armchair

Part 5

33

Questions 21–25

For each question, choose the correct answer.

You will hear Paul and Donna talking about summer jobs.
What job does each person have?

Example:

Donna   B

People

21   Clare   ☐

22   Kevin   ☐

23   Paul   ☐

24   Tony   ☐

25   Katherine   ☐

Job

A   cleaner

B   waiter

C   journalist

D   factory worker

E   tour guide

F   farm worker

G   receptionist

H   teacher

You now have six minutes to write your answers on the answer sheet.

Test 5 SPEAKING

You are Candidate B. Answer the questions.

🎧 34–35

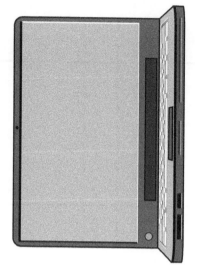

Do you like these different presents for a teenager?

Audio scripts and Model answers on pages 167–223.

Test 6

TEST 6 READING AND WRITING

Part 1

Questions 1–6

For each question, choose the correct answer.

1

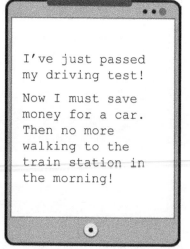

I've just passed my driving test!

Now I must save money for a car. Then no more walking to the train station in the morning!

How will the person probably go to work tomorrow?

A by train

B by car

C on foot

2

Road closed because of roadworks.
Monday 28 September –
Thursday 1 October
Use Broad Street.

A You can use the road only during these dates.

B Broad Street is closed during these dates.

C You can use Broad Street during these dates.

3

SPECIAL OFFER!

**All laptops over £500 come with a free printer.
Offer ends Friday!**

A All laptops come with a free printer.

B All laptops in the shop cost more than £500.

C If you spend more than £500 on a laptop, you get a printer.

4

Dance class
finishes at 17:30,
not 17.00 tomorrow
so don't wait for
me outside the
library. I'll meet
you at the cinema
instead.

Where do they usually meet?

A at the dance class

B outside the library

C at the cinema

5

Choose your seat when you book online or before your flight for your 10% discount.

A You must choose your seat before you get on your flight.

B If you choose your seat in advance, you pay less.

C You pay less when you book a flight online.

6

To: Josh
From: Mum
Anna phoned. She forgot to tell you – the concert is the 6th, not 5th. Let her know if you can go.

A Josh didn't know that the date of the concert had changed.

B Anna has forgotten what date the concert is on.

C Anna needs to tell Josh what day the concert is on.

Part 2

Questions 7–13

For each question, choose the correct answer.

		Liza	Hannah	Paula
7	Who says that her feelings were different from her parents'?	A	B	C
8	Whose says that something very unusual happened?	A	B	C
9	Who thought that the weather would become bad?	A	B	C
10	Who had everything she needed when the weather became bad?	A	B	C
11	Who describes an activity her family does a lot?	A	B	C
12	Who says that she couldn't leave her home because of the bad weather?	A	B	C
13	Who was in danger because of the bad weather?	A	B	C

Bad weather

Liza

I live in the north of Finland. We're used to snow there, but one year we had a very bad snowstorm. When we woke up one morning the snow was nearly as high as the house. It covered our car and our garden, and we couldn't open our front door. We didn't have any electricity, and it was dark and cold. Luckily, we were prepared, and we had a radio with batteries, a torch and warm clothes. For me it was like an adventure, but my mum and dad were very worried.

Hannah

My family and I often go sailing, but last summer we had a bad experience. The day began well. It was a hot and sunny so we decided to take the boat out. An hour later the weather changed very suddenly. The wind became stronger, clouds covered the sun, it started to rain and the sea became very rough. I thought we were going to die. Luckily, after a few hours the storm passed, but it was the scariest day of my life.

Paula

My village is near the sea, and a few winters ago something very strange happened. The wind became very strong and big waves started crashing over the harbour edge onto the road. Overnight, the temperature dropped so low that the seawater turned into ice. The next day the sea looked like a giant ice rink. There was also ice on the roads and the cars. Luckily nobody was hurt, but it was the strangest weather I've ever experienced.

Part 3

Questions 14–18

For each question, choose the correct answer.

Too much plastic

by Paula Jones

Plastic is everywhere: in our streets, in the countryside, in rivers, in seas and in oceans. In the UK, over 13 billion plastic bottles are used every year. The good news is that more and more people are recycling plastic and there are also some clever ways to use it.

Roads are usually made of asphalt, but in some countries like the USA and the UK, engineers have started to use plastic to make new roads. First, they collect the plastic, wash it and dry it. Then they cut it into small pieces and heat it to about 170°C. After that, they mix it with hot asphalt and use it to make the road surface. This way of making roads is more difficult than the usual way, but the plastic and asphalt mixture is harder and better than asphalt only.

How about wearing a pair of trainers made from recycled plastic bottles? Some well-known sports companies use six to eleven plastic bottles to make one pair of trainers. This means that fewer plastic bottles are thrown away, and they end up on people's feet, not in the ocean!

Plastic can be recycled in other clever ways too. It is used to make rubbish bins, toys, tables and chairs, sleeping bags, backpacks and hundreds of other things. One clothes company cuts it into very small pieces to make clothes. Believe it or not, the England women's national football team wears a kit made from recycled bottles!

14 What is happening in the UK that is good news?

    A Plastic can be used in clever ways.

    B Over 13 billion plastic bottles are used every year.

    C There are a lot of clever people there.

15 Which of these sentences is true?

    A Roads are made of plastic all over the world.

    B Engineers usually make plastic roads in the UK and the USA.

    C In the past, roads weren't made of plastic.

16 Asphalt and plastic roads

    A are not easy to make.

    B are better when they are heated to 170°C.

    C are not as hard as roads that have only asphalt.

17 Some famous companies

    A make sports shoes using rubbish.

    B throw away fewer plastic bottles than others.

    C use six to eleven plastic bottles to make one shoe.

18 The writer says that you can use plastic to make

    A footballs.

    B camping equipment.

    C rubbish bins and jewellery.

Part 4

Questions 19–24

For each question, choose the correct answer.

The festival of light

Diwali is an **(19)** .... Indian festival. It takes place every year in October or November during the autumn, and it lasts for five days. The word 'Diwali' **(20)** .... from Sanskrit, an ancient Indian language, and it **(21)** .... 'row of lights'. During the festival, people clean their homes, decorate them with lights and oil lamps, and enjoy **(22)** .... time with friends and family. They give each other gifts and sweets, eat delicious food, **(23)** .... fireworks and wear new clothes. Many people in the UK also celebrate Diwali. In the city of Leicester, thousands of people go out into the **(24)** .... to enjoy light shows, music and dancing.

---

19 **A** excellent   **B** interested   **C** important

20 **A** comes   **B** goes   **C** looks

21 **A** seems   **B** means   **C** looks

22 **A** making   **B** spending   **C** doing

23 **A** listen   **B** look   **C** watch

24 **A** streets   **B** areas   **C** paths

Part 5

Questions 25–30

For each question, write the correct answer.
Write **one** word for each gap.

Example: | 0 | *a* |

> **EMAIL**
>
> From: Sofia
>
> To: Lucia
>
> I've had **(0)** .... great week! I've been on holiday
> in the United Arab Emirates. We went to an amazing
> place today. Have you **(25)** .... heard of the Mall
> of the Emirates in Dubai? You don't get bored here
> **(26)** .... there's so much to see and do. There are
> over 700 shops **(27)** .... more than 100 places to
> eat. There's also a theme park in the building. It's got
> a 4D cinema and a rollercoaster. I've **(28)** .... on
> it twice – it's really fast! But **(29)** .... best thing in
> the mall is the ski slope! I'm going there tomorrow. I'll
> send you **(30)** .... photos later.

Part 6

Question 31

You want to play badminton on Saturday with your English friend, Amy.
Write an email to Amy.

In your email:

- say where you want to play.
- say what time you want to meet.
- ask Amy what she wants to do afterwards.

Write **25 words** or more.

Write the note on your answer sheet.

Part 7

Questions 32

Look at the three pictures.
Write the story shown in the pictures.
Write **35 words** or more.

Write the story on your answer sheet.

TEST 6 LISTENING

Part 1

Questions 1–5

For each question, choose the correct answer.

---

1 Where were the sunglasses the last time Mark saw them?

A

B

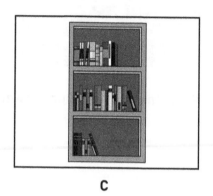

C

2 Where did the man see the ad for the concert?

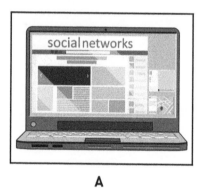

A

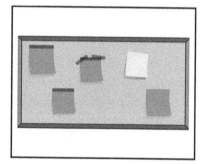

B

C

3 Who is Simon?

A

B

C

4 What job does the woman want help with?

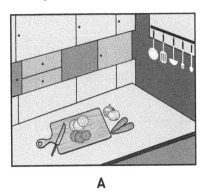

A

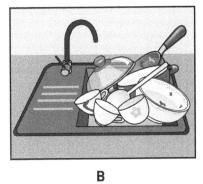

B

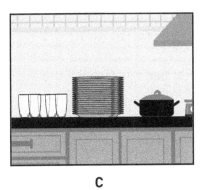

C

5 When might the next bus arrive?

A

B

C

Part 2

37

Questions 6–10

For each question, write the correct answer in the gap. **Write one word or a number or a date or a time.**

You will hear a tour guide talking about a boat tour in Venice.

Boat tour	
Where:	Venice, Italy
Number of islands:	**(6)** ....
Length of the Grand Canal:	nearly **(7)** ....kilometres
Number of bridges in Venice:	**(8)** ....
Duration of tour:	**(9)** .... minutes
Buildings along the Grand Canal:	palaces, churches, museums, **(10)** .... market

38

Part 3

Questions 11–15

For each question, choose the correct answer.

___

You will hear Lisa talking to her friend Robin about finding a place to live.

11 Lisa

    A has found possible places to live online.

    B has talked to someone about places to live.

    C has decided to live in a university flat in the city centre.

12 Which sentence is true?

    A The university has 20 apartment buildings in the city centre.

    B One apartment building in the city centre has nine flats.

    C A number of students live in each of the flats in the city centre.

13 Howard House

    A isn't far from the university.

    B is too expensive for Lisa.

    C has two canteens.

14 In Morgan House

    A students can't cook their own meals.

    B students have to share the bathrooms.

    C there are 25 students.

15 What does Lisa think about Howard House and Morgan House?

    A She isn't sure which one she will prefer.

    B She won't like the other students who live there.

    C She thinks they are very nice places to live.

Part 4

Questions 16–20

39

For each question, choose the correct answer.

___

16 You will hear two friends talking about the weather.
   What is the weather going to be like tomorrow?

   A sunny

   B windy

   C rainy

17 You will hear a man talking to his friend on the phone.
   Why is he angry?

   A There is a problem with his suit.

   B He lost all his money.

   C The dry cleaner's didn't give him his suit.

18 You will hear a woman talking to her friend about work.
   Why is she unhappy?

   A She has to work at the weekend.

   B She works too many hours.

   C She has to work in the evening.

19 You will hear a man talking to his friend about where he lives.
   What does he say about it?

   A It is a noisy place to live.

   B He doesn't like the people he lives with.

   C It takes a long time to get to work.

20 You will hear two friends talking about a sports centre.
   Which sport is the woman going to do?

   A tennis

   B volleyball

   C football

Part 5

Questions 21–25

For each question, choose the correct answer.

You will hear Charlie talking to his friend Evie about visiting his family.
What gift did he buy for each person?

Example:

Grandmother ☐ C

People

21 grandfather ☐

22 mother ☐

23 father ☐

24 brother ☐

25 sister ☐

Gifts

A digital radio

B book

C gloves

D backpack

E wallet

F football shirt

G jewellery

H camera

You now have six minutes to write your answers on the answer sheet.

Test 6 SPEAKING

You are Candidate B. Answer the question.

41–42

Do you like these different outdoor activities?

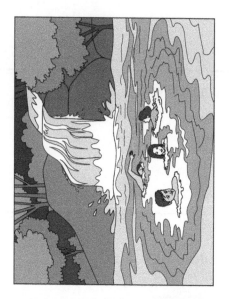

Audio scripts and Model answers on pages 167–223.

Test 7

TEST 7 READING AND WRITING

Part 1

Questions 1–6

For each question, choose the correct answer.

1

FOR RENT

3-bedroomed house
£750 per month,
bills included
Quiet location
No pets

A The cost of renting the house is more than £750 per month.

B You can't live in the house if you have a dog or a cat.

C You must be quiet to rent this house.

2

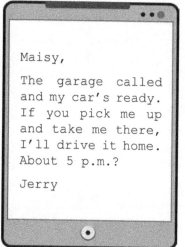

Maisy,

The garage called and my car's ready. If you pick me up and take me there, I'll drive it home. About 5 p.m.?

Jerry

A Jerry wants Maisy to give him a lift to the garage.

B Jerry wants Maisy to help him take his car to the garage.

C The garage wants Maisy to pick Jerry up.

3

SALE!

30% off all sports equipment
15% off sports clothing
Offer ends Tuesday

A After Tuesday, sports equipment and sports clothing will be cheaper.

B You can save more on a basketball than on basketball shoes.

C On Tuesday, sports equipment and clothing will be more expensive.

4

> **CLOSED**
> **We're sorry to say**
> **because of illness**
> **we are closed until**
> **further notice.**

A The shop is closed and there is more information on another notice.

B The shop is closed because the owner is in hospital.

C The shop is closed and they will give more information in the future.

5

> Justin,
>
> I've just gone to the shops. I've left a key under the bin. Go in and make yourself comfortable. Back in 30 minutes.
>
> Flo

A Justin is visiting Flo.

B Flo wants Justin to leave her key under the bin.

C Justin's key is under the bin.

6

> **To:** Matilda
> **From:** Rod
>
> Hi Matilda,
>
> Is there any chance you could work on Saturday? Timothy wants a day off. I can pay you double.
>
> Rod

A Matilda couldn't work on Saturday.

B Rod wants Timothy to have a day off.

C Rod wants Matilda to work instead of Timothy.

Part 2

Questions 7–13

For each question, choose the correct answer.

		Lloyd	Emma	Amna
7	Who didn't study art?	A	B	C
8	Who doesn't earn all their money from their art?	A	B	C
9	Who won a prize for their art?	A	B	C
10	Who has a family member who is also an artist?	A	B	C
11	Whose art shows everyday life?	A	B	C
12	Who doesn't paint?	A	B	C
13	Who has been a full-time artist for the longest time?	A	B	C

Young artists

Lloyd

I've worked as a full-time artist for five years. After leaving art college, I did some part-time jobs working as a waiter and washing dishes in a restaurant. But then I started to sell some paintings so I gave up my other jobs. Most of my paintings are of city street scenes – they are full of people just living their lives. People buy my paintings because they can see places they know in them.

Emma

I'm still very early on in my career as an artist. I trained as a doctor and my art is slowly changing from a hobby to a job. I work with wood and metal. I'm interested in showing my feelings through my work. It's very personal to me. Maybe that's why I don't sell very much. I still work as a doctor two days a week. My parents are very proud of me, especially my mother, who draws a lot.

Amna

My parents wanted me to be a doctor, like them, but I had no interest in studying medicine. I first became interested in art when I was at school. I came first in a competition and I was given a painting set, and I have never looked back! I was lucky enough to get a place at university on a course which helped me improve my painting skills. They're actually quite good now. I've managed to earn enough money from my art for the past two years, so I don't need to do other work.

Part 3

Questions 14–18

For each question, choose the correct answer.

Little girl saves mother

A little girl from Newton has become the most famous person in town. Frances Brown, who is starting school next year, called 999 when her mother, Lisa, fell down the stairs. The emergency services immediately sent an ambulance to her house.

'She's an amazing little girl!' said a doctor. 'She knew that she had to call 999 to speak to someone who could help. She gave her name and her address, and she described what the problem was. She said her mother had just got out of bed and had fallen down the stairs. She said that her mum was sleeping, but there was something wrong. She looked after her mum until help arrived.'

When the ambulance arrived at the Browns' house, they found out that Lisa, aged 30, is expecting her second child. The doctors kept Lisa in hospital for 24 hours to check that she was all right before allowing her to go home the next morning.

When Lisa found out what her daughter did she told friends and family. Then the local newspaper heard the story. Frances's father, Liam, aged 32 and a teacher at the local school, said: 'Frances's quick thinking saved her mother's life. Lisa is careful around the house, but accidents happen.'

Lisa is going to have a baby in two months, and she thinks this is why she fell down the stairs. 'I'm so big now that I can't see my feet!' she said. 'I can't wait to give Frances a baby brother.'

14 Frances

    A is still at school.

    B has just started school.

    C isn't old enough to go to school.

15 On the telephone, Frances

    A told the emergency services where she lived.

    B told the emergency services that she needed an ambulance.

    C told the emergency services that her mother was in bed.

16 Lisa

    A didn't stay in hospital.

    B stayed in hospital for one night.

    C went to hospital but returned home that night.

17 Liam thinks

    A Lisa might have died.

    B Lisa should start thinking more quickly.

    C Lisa should be more careful around the house.

18 Frances

    A has two brothers.

    B already has a brother.

    C is going to have a brother soon.

Part 4

Questions 19–24

For each question, choose the correct answer.

Ella Fitzgerald

Ella Fitzgerald, the great American jazz singer, was born in Virginia in 1917. She **(19)** .... to New York when she was a young child.

When Ella was fifteen her mother died, and she went to live with her aunt. This was a hard time in her life and she got into **(20)** .... with the police. She **(21)** .... money from singing on the street and people started to notice her.

In 1934 she won first prize in a competition, and she **(22)** .... a well-known band. By 1938 she was famous and her songs were the best-selling recordings of the time.

Fitzgerald starred in films and appeared in many television shows. She also went on **(23)** .... around the world. She died in 1996. In the **(24)** .... of many people, she is the greatest ever jazz singer.

19	**A** kept	**B** changed	**C** moved
20	**A** trouble	**B** problem	**C** danger
21	**A** won	**B** made	**C** took
22	**A** became	**B** played	**C** joined
23	**A** tour	**B** guide	**C** concert
24	**A** idea	**B** opinion	**C** thought

Part 5

Questions 25–30

For each question, write the correct answer.
Write **one** word for each gap.

Example: | 0 | *you* |

> **EMAIL**
>
> From: Jonathan
>
> To: Peter
>
> Dear Peter,
>
> I hope **(0)** .... are well. I am writing to tell you some news. Amanda and I are getting married in **(25)** .... summer and we **(26)** .... love you to come. We have lots of plans! The wedding **(27)** .... be in June. We are **(28)** .... to have a big party afterwards at my parents' house. We have invited hundreds **(29)** .... guests. I know you live far away, but the house has a spare room and you can stay here for a few days.
>
> Please **(30)** .... me know if you can come.
>
> Jonathan

Part 6

Question 31

You arranged a time to meet your English friend Mark at a café but you didn't go.
Write an email to your friend.

In your email:

- say you are sorry you didn't go.
- say why you missed the meeting.
- suggest a new time to meet.

Write **25 words** or more.

Write the email on your answer sheet.

Part 7

Question 32

Look at the three pictures.
Write the story shown in the pictures.
Write **35 words** or more.

Write the story on your answer sheet.

TEST 7 LISTENING

Part 1

Questions 1–5

For each question, choose the correct answer.

---

1   What time will the man pick up the woman?

A

B

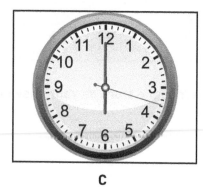

C

2   Where will they meet?

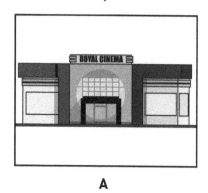

A

B

C

3   What sort of holiday will they go on?

A

B

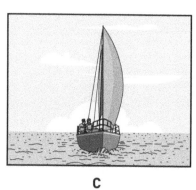

C

4 What musical instrument will she learn to play?

A

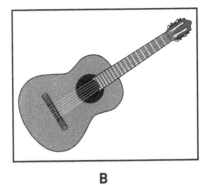

B

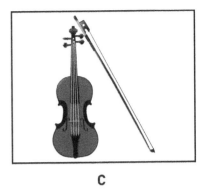

C

5 What date is the man's appointment with the dentist?

A

B

C

Part 2

44

Questions 6–10

For each question, write the correct answer in the gap. **Write one word or a number or a date or a time.**

You will hear a speaker giving information to university students about evening language courses.

Language Classes at the University Language Centre

Languages:	English, Italian, French, Russian, Spanish
Courses start:	**(6)** .... week of October
Cost of courses (except English):	**(7)** £..............
Cost of second language course:	**(8)** £..............
Number of lessons per course:	**(9)** English: ....; other languages: 18
All students should bring:	**(10)** .... and pen or pencil

---

Part 3

45

Questions 11–15

For each question, choose the correct answer.

You will hear Paul talking to his friend, Debbie, about his new job.

11 Paul

    A misses his old colleagues.

    B had problems with his old colleagues.

    C didn't meet new people in his old job.

12 In his new job, Paul

    A completes documents.

    B speaks to customers.

    C has to drive a car.

13 When there is a delay,

    A people can't rent a car.

    B Paul sometimes gets angry.

    C some customers aren't happy.

14 What does Paul say about the people who work with him?

    A More people work outside the office than inside the office.

    B The people outside the office work more than the people inside.

    C The people who work in the office get the cars ready.

15 Paul

    A gets more money at his new job than his old job.

    B got more money at his old job than he gets now.

    C is new at his job but he has more money now.

Part 4

Questions 16–20

46

For each question, choose the correct answer.

---

16 You will hear a woman talking about her day.
Where did she go?

    A to the museum

    B to the library

    C to the cinema

17 You will hear a man talking.
What has he lost?

    A his money

    B his keys

    C his car

18 You will hear two friends talking.
What will they do this afternoon?

    A watch a football game

    B play tennis

    C watch a film

19 You will hear two friends talking.
What will they have for dinner?

    A curry

    B fish and chips

    C pizza

20 You will hear a man talking in a shop.
What is he looking at?

    A televisions

    B laptops

    C radios

Part 5

47

Questions 21–25

For each question, choose the correct answer.

You will hear Dean and Kylie planning the final week of their holiday.
What activity will they do on each day?

Example:

Monday   B

Days

21	Tuesday	☐
22	Wednesday	☐
23	Thursday	☐
24	Friday	☐
25	Saturday	☐

Activities

A shopping

B museum

C water park

D guided tour

E boat trip

F fish market

G palace

H zoo

You now have six minutes to write your answers on the answer sheet.

Test 7 SPEAKING

You are Candidate B. Answer the question.

48–49

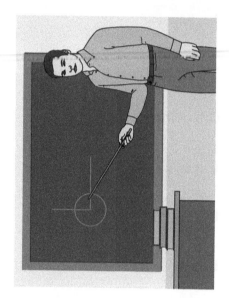

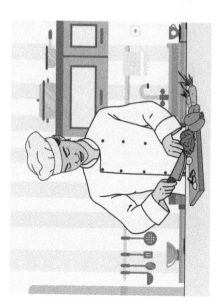

Do you like these different jobs?

Audio scripts and Model answers on pages 167–223.

Test 8

TEST 8 READING AND WRITING

Part 1

Questions 1–6

For each question, choose the correct answer.

1

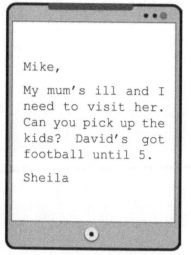

Mike,

My mum's ill and I need to visit her. Can you pick up the kids? David's got football until 5.

Sheila

A Sheila wants Mike to get David a football.

B Mike's mum is ill.

C Sheila needs help with the children.

2

WAIT HERE

Please take a ticket and wait for your number to come up.

A You might have to wait.

B If you take a ticket, you don't need to wait.

C When your number comes up, you should take a ticket.

3

Hi Maria,

My car's broken down, so I'm getting the bus! I'll be there soon. Sorry! Please order me something simple, like a sandwich.

Heather

A Maria's car is not working.

B Maria is waiting for Heather.

C Heather wants Maria to have a sandwich.

4

SCHOOL GYM
No outside shoes
No ball games
Equipment only for use
with your teacher.

A Children can play football in the gym.

B Children cannot wear shoes in the gym.

C Children cannot use the equipment without their teacher.

5

To: Grace

From: Keira

Dear Grace,

Poppy's away and I'm the only receptionist. Can you take her place until lunchtime when it will be quieter?

Regards,
Keira

A Keira is too busy at work.

B Keira wants to meet Grace for lunch.

C Keira wants to have a quiet lunch.

6

Hi everyone,

The sports hall isn't available this Friday, so basketball training will take place on Thursday! Same time and place.

Tony

A The time of day for basketball training has changed.

B Basketball training will not take place in the sports hall this week.

C Basketball training is usually on Friday.

Part 2

Questions 7–13

For each question, choose the correct answer.

		Claude	Polly	Stan
7	Who says children need to feel comfortable at school?	A	B	C
8	Who says what they like doing outside work?	A	B	C
9	Whose pupils have to pass important exams?	A	B	C
10	Who enjoys watching their pupils change?	A	B	C
11	Who didn't plan to be a teacher?	A	B	C
12	Who was surprised to find out how much work teachers have to do?	A	B	C
13	Who talks about the subject they teach?	A	B	C

Three teachers tell us why they love their jobs

A Claudia

My mum and dad were teachers so it's not surprising that I became one. I saw how happy they were in their jobs and I always thought teaching was a possibility for me. But I didn't think it would be such hard work. During term time there is absolutely no time for any personal evening activities in the week. Luckily, we get good holidays and I love travelling when I get the chance.

B Polly

I did a teacher training course in college and now I work in a school with children aged four to eleven. I love seeing them growing up in front of my eyes! I teach kids in their first year at school. At the beginning of the year they are usually shy and quiet, but I do everything I can to make them feel relaxed and happy. If they aren't happy and relaxed, they aren't going to learn. I'm glad tests aren't important for my pupils.

C Stan

I teach history to children over the age of sixteen. Most of them work very hard because they want to get good marks and get into the university of their choice. I love discussing things with them and helping them understand the links between what has happened in the past and things that are happening now. I never thought I would be a teacher – I only turned to it when I was looking for a job after university – and I love it!

Part 3

Questions 14–18

For each question, choose the correct answer.

School counts the cost of storm

When children and parents arrived at school in the small village of Brownston yesterday morning, they were surprised to see the head teacher standing outside the front of the school. The school gates were closed, because a tree had fallen onto the roof of the school hall and a number of windows were broken. A storm the night before had made school buildings unsafe, so the children were sent home until further notice.

Justine Cram, a mother with two young children at the school, said that she was unhappy with the way the head teacher sent the children home. 'I have to cancel all my work appointments today. My customers won't be pleased, but I have to stay at home to look after my daughters,' she said. 'Children should be in school every day! The head teacher needs to think again about closing. He should find a safe place to teach the children until they can use the buildings again.'

Richard Thomas, the head teacher, explained that he had no choice but to send the children home. 'The storm happened in the early hours of Monday morning, just a few hours before school starts. When I arrived, I immediately decided it was not a safe place for children to be in. I know parents are unhappy that the school is closed, but if their children or members of staff were hurt because of the problems, that would be worse.'

Mr Thomas hopes to open the school again by Thursday.

14 School children and their parents

    A do not usually see the head teacher standing outside the front of the school.

    B surprised the head teacher when they arrived at school.

    C arrived at school at the same time as the head teacher.

15 The children and their parents

    A couldn't open the school gates because a tree had fallen.

    B watched a tree fall and break several windows.

    C could see that the storm had caused problems.

16 Justine Cram

    A couldn't go to work because the school was closed.

    B wants to make an appointment to talk to head teacher.

    C thinks the school is safe enough for the children.

17 Mr Thomas believes

    A people should think before closing a school.

    B the storm happened too early in the morning.

    C he was right to send the children home.

18 The school

    A will certainly open again this week.

    B might open on Thursday or Friday.

    C will not open before next Monday.

Part 4

Questions 19–24

For each question, choose the correct answer.

The American black bear

Black bears are the smallest American bears. They are also the ones that are found across the biggest **(19)** .... in North America.

They eat plants, insects, fish and meat, but when the seasons change and they **(20)** .... from place to place, they find different kinds of food to eat. They usually live in forests, but they leave the shelter of the trees to **(21)** .... food. Sometimes they go into towns because they find food more easily there, often in rubbish bins. They don't often hurt people, but they can be dangerous. They leave marks on trees **(22)** .... their teeth. This is a way of leaving **(23)** .... to other bears.

There are many American black bears and scientists do not think they are in **(24)** .... of dying out.

19	**A** room	**B** space	**C** area
20	**A** move	**B** arrive	**C** leave
21	**A** look after	**B** look for	**C** look at
22	**A** working	**B** using	**C** brushing
23	**A** words	**B** letters	**C** messages
24	**A** pain	**B** trouble	**C** danger

Part 5

Questions 25–30

For each question, write the correct answer.
Write **one** word for each gap.

Example: | **0** | *was* |

EMAIL

From: | Steven

To: | Mum and Dad

Dear Mum and Dad,

It **(0)** .... lovely to see you last weekend, but I think I forgot to put some things **(25)** .... my suitcase when I packed.

First, **(26)** .... you seen my green jumper? **(27)** .... last time I saw it, it was on the end of my bed. Also, I think I forgot to pack my book. It's exciting, so I really want **(28)** .... back quickly. **(29)** .... you send the jumper and the book to me as soon as possible?

If you send them by post, I'll get them by the end **(30)** .... the week. Thanks!

Love,
Steven

Part 6

Question 31

Your friend Eddie invited you to his house last weekend.
Write an email to Eddie.

In your email:

- say thank you for inviting you to his house
- say what you enjoyed most about the weekend
- say you would like to meet again soon

Write **25 words** or more.

Write the email on your answer sheet.

Part 7

Question 32

Look at the three pictures.
Write the story shown in the pictures.
Write **35 words** or more.

  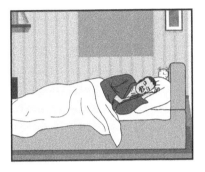

Write the story on your answer sheet.

TEST 8 LISTENING

Part 1

Questions 1–5

For each question, choose the correct answer.

---

1   How long will they park for?

  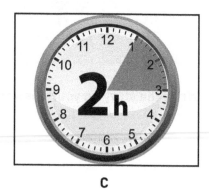

A   B   C

2   What else will they have in their picnic?

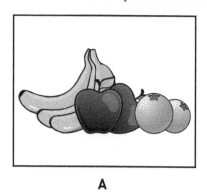 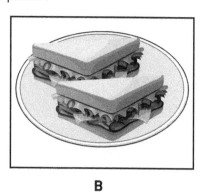 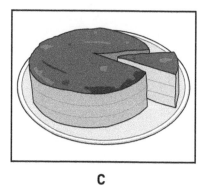

A   B   C

3   What will they take to hospital for Jemima?

 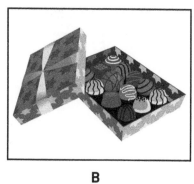 

A   B   C

4 Where does Alex live?

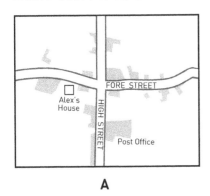  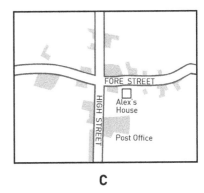

A **B** **C**

5 How much will Nicola pay for her hotel room?

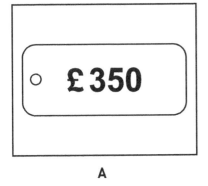 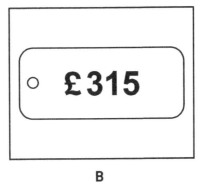 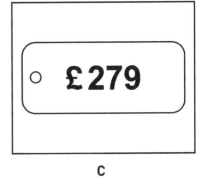

A **B** **C**

Part 2

51

Questions 6–10

For each question, write the correct answer in the gap. **Write one word or a number or a date or a time.**

You will hear a speaker giving information at the start of a coach trip to London.

Coach trip to London

Journey to London:	2 hours
Free time in London:	from 10.15 a.m. until **(6)** .... p.m.
Discount:	**(7)** ....% at Kings and Queens Shopping Centre
To get a discount, show your coach	**(8)** ....
Please look after your purses and	**(9)** ....
Michaela's personal mobile phone number:	**(10)** 0777...............

52

Part 3

Questions 11–15

For each question, choose the correct answer.

You will hear Vivien and Tom talking about their meals last night.

11 The table in Vivien's restaurant was

    A too big.

    B too small.

    C too round.

12 Vivien's restaurant

    A had special food for people like Monica.

    B had a lot of dishes on the menu.

    C didn't have vegetarian dishes.

13 At Vivien's restaurant, Mark

    A changed his order.

    B ordered chicken.

    C had steak.

14 At Tom's restaurant,

    A the dessert was the best part of the meal.

    B everything was delicious, but not the dessert.

    C the food was delicious, but the dessert wasn't as good as the rest of the meal.

15 Tom

    A paid too much for his meal.

    B paid less than the full price for his meal.

    C fixed the problem with the bill after half an hour.

Part 4

53

Questions 16–20

For each question, choose the correct answer.

---

16 You will hear two friends talking.
    Why can't the man play football this afternoon?

   A He has a bad foot.

   B He has to work.

   C He has to go to the dentist.

17 You will hear a man talking.
    What animal did he see at the zoo?

   A an elephant

   B a bear

   C a tiger

18 You will hear two friends talking.
    Where have they been?

   A to the library

   B shopping

   C to the cinema

19 You will hear a woman talking.
    Where does her friend live?

   A in a city

   B in a village

   C by the sea

20 You will hear two friends talking about cooking dinner.
    What will the man do?

   A wash the vegetables

   B cut the vegetables

   C cook the vegetables

Part 5

54

Questions 21–25

For each question, choose the correct answer.

You will hear two people talking about their families.
What activities do their children like?

Example:

George | D |

Children

21 Henry   ☐

22 Edward   ☐

23 Annabel ☐

24 Sophie   ☐

25 Ellie   ☐

Activities

A playing board games

B going to the cinema

C visiting art exhibitions

D reading

E going to the theatre

F playing video games

G dancing

H playing the electric guitar

You now have six minutes to write your answers on the answer sheet.

Test 8 SPEAKING

You are Candidate B. Answer the question.

55–56

Do you like these different ways of getting the news?

Audio scripts and Model answers on pages 167–223.

Mini-dictionary

 Here are some of the more difficult words from the practice tests. Definitions and examples are from *Collins COBUILD Dictionaries.*

TEST 1

block /blɒk/ **(blocks, blocking, blocked)** VERB to stop someone or something from passing along a road • *A tree fell down and blocked the road.*

choice /tʃɔɪs/ **(choices)** NOUN a situation when there are several things and you can choose the one you want • *It comes in a choice of colours.*

fine /faɪn/ ADJECTIVE satisfactory or acceptable • *Everything is going to be just fine.*
(fines) NOUN money that someone has to pay because they have done something wrong • *She got a £300 fine for driving dangerously.*

including /ɪnˈkluːdɪŋ/ PREPOSITION You use **including** to introduce examples of people or things that are part of the group of people or things that you are talking about. • *Thousands were at the concert, including many women and children.*

love /lʌv/ NOUN If two people **fall in love**, they start to love each other in a romantic way. • *Maria fell in love with Danny as soon as she met him.*

manufacture /ˌmænjʊˈfæktʃə/ **(manufactures, manufacturing, manufactured)** VERB to make something in a factory • *The company manufactures plastics.*

off /ɒf/ ADVERB away from work or school • *She took the day off.*

ordinary /ˈɔːdɪnri/ ADJECTIVE normal and not special or different • *These are just ordinary people living their lives.*

romantic /rəʊˈmæntɪk/ ADJECTIVE used when you are talking about love and romance • *It is a lovely romantic film.*

strict /strɪkt/ ADJECTIVE that you must obey completely • *The school's rules are very strict.*

on time /ɒn taɪm/ PHRASE If someone or something is **on time**, it is not late or early. • *The train arrived at the station on time at eleven thirty.*

widely /ˈwaɪdli/ ADVERB You use **widely** if something includes a large number of different things or people. • *Broadband is not as widely available in rural areas.*

TEST 2

apply /əˈplaɪ/ **(applies, applying, applied)** VERB to write a letter or write on a form in order to ask for something such as a job • *I am applying for a new job.*

asleep /əˈsliːp/ ADJECTIVE If you **fall asleep**, you start sleeping. • *Sam soon fell asleep.*

author /ˈɔːθə/ **(authors)** NOUN a person whose job is writing books • *He is Japan's best-selling author.*

beauty /ˈbjuːti/ NOUN the quality of being beautiful • *The hotel is in an area of natural beauty.*

cliff /klɪf/ **(cliffs)** NOUN a high area of land with a very steep side next to the sea • *The car rolled over the edge of a cliff.*

exchange student /ɪkˈstʃeɪndʒ ˈstjuːdənt/ NOUN **(exchange students)** a student who goes to school in another country, while a student from that country goes to school in the country of the first student

frightening /ˈfraɪtənɪŋ/ ADJECTIVE making you feel afraid, anxious or nervous • *It was a very frightening experience.*

galaxy /ˈɡæləksi/ **(galaxies)** NOUN a very large group of stars and planets • *Astronomers have discovered a distant galaxy.*

homestay /ˈhəʊmˌsteɪ/ **(homestays)** NOUN A **homestay** is the time living as a guest in someone's home in another country. • *One of my favourite trips was a homestay in Thailand.*

ID card /aɪ diː kɑːʳd/ **(ID cards)** NOUN **ID card** is short for 'identity card'. • *Don't leave bank or ID cards lying around.*

identity card /aɪˈdentɪti kɑːʳd/ **(identity cards)** NOUN An **identity card** is a card with information about a person on it. The abbreviation 'ID card' is also used. • *Computers check the identity cards of everyone coming in.*

interactive /ˌɪntəˈræktɪv/ **ADJECTIVE** used to talk about something that allows direct communication between itself and the user • *Press the red button on your interactive TV to vote.*

kayaking /ˈkaɪækɪŋ/ **NOUN** the sport of using and racing a small narrow boat like a canoe • *They went kayaking in Canada.*

label /ˈleɪbəl/ **(labels, labelling, labelled)** **VERB** to attach a piece of paper or plastic to an object to give information about it • *All foods must be clearly labelled.*

light pollution /laɪt pəluːʃən/ **NOUN** the glow from street and house lights that makes it difficult to see stars • *With no light pollution, the sky at night is very clear.*

look through /lʊk θruː/ **(looks through, looking through, looked through)** **PHRASAL VERB** If you **look through** a group of things, you look at each one so that you can find or choose the one that you want. • *Peter starts looking through the mall as soon as the door shuts.*

main /meɪn/ **ADJECTIVE** most important • *The main reason I came today was to say sorry.*

nearby /ˌnɪəˈbaɪ/ **ADVERB** only a short distance away • *Her sister lives nearby.*

northwest /ˌnɔːθˈwest/ **(northwests)** **ADJECTIVE** in the direction that is between north and west • *I live in northwest London.*

photo album /foʊtoʊ ælbəm/ **(photo albums)** **NOUN** a book that has lots of photographs in it • *He brought out the family photo album.*

rarely /ˈreəˈli/ **ADVERB** If something **rarely** happens, it does not happen very often. • *I very rarely wear a coat in summer.*

reduce /rɪˈdjuːs/ **(reduces, reducing, reduced)** **VERB** to make something smaller or less • *Exercise reduces the risks of heart disease.*

sight /saɪt/ **(sights)** **NOUN** something that is interesting to see • *Seeing the Northern Lights is an amazing sight.*

smartly /ˈsmɑːtli/ **ADVERB** in a clean and tidy way • *He is a tall, smartly dressed young man.*

southwest /ˌsaʊθˈwest/ **NOUN** the direction that is between south and west • *He lives about 500 miles to the southwest of Johannesburg.*

souvenir /ˌsuːvəˈnɪə/ **(souvenirs)** **NOUN** something that you buy or keep to remind you of a place or an event • *He had a shop selling souvenirs and postcards.*

TEST 3

audience /ˈɔːdiəns/ **(audiences)** **NOUN** all the people who are watching or listening to a performance, a film or a television programme • *There was a TV audience of 35 million.*

culture /ˈkʌltʃə/ **(cultures)** **NOUN** the way of life, the traditions and beliefs of a particular group of people • *I live in the city among people from different cultures.*

education /ˌedʒʊˈkeɪʃən/ **NOUN** teaching and learning • *My children's education is important to me.*

on hold /ɒn həʊld/ **PHRASE** If you put something **on hold**, you decide not to do it, deal with it, or change it now, but to leave it until later. • *He put his career on hold until he had moved house.*

opportunity /ˌɒpəˈtjuːnɪti/ **(opportunities)** **NOUN** a situation in which it is possible for you to do something that you want to do • *I had an opportunity to go to New York and study.*

run /rʌn/ **(runs, running, ran)** **VERB** to be in charge of a business or an activity • *She runs a restaurant in San Francisco.*

soldier /ˈsəʊldʒə/ **(soldiers)** **NOUN** a member of an army • *The colour photographs made the soldiers look much younger.*

tourism /ˈtʊərɪzəm/ **NOUN** the business of providing hotels, restaurants, trips and activities for people who are on holiday • *Tourism is the island's main industry.*

war /wɔː/ **(wars)** **NOUN** a period of fighting between countries or groups • *He spent part of the war in France.*

TEST 4

apply /əˈplaɪ/ **(applies, applying, applied)** **VERB** If you **apply to** something, you write on a form so that you can join it. • *She applied to join the police.*

archeologist /ˌɑːkiˈɒlədʒɪst/ **(archeologists)** **NOUN** a person whose job is to study the past by examining the things that remain, such as buildings and tools • *Archeologists discovered ancient buildings in Mexico City.*

architect /ˈɑːkɪtekt/ **(architects)** **NOUN** a person whose job is to design buildings • *The buildings were designed by local architects.*

connection /kəˈnekʃən/ **(connections)** NOUN a way of joining one thing, especially a computer, with another • *You'll need a fast internet connection to view this site.*

costume /ˈkɒstjuːm/ **(costumes)** NOUN a set of clothes that someone wears in a performance • *The costumes and scenery were designed by my partner.*

disappointed /ˌdɪsəˈpɔɪntɪd/ ADJECTIVE sad because something has not happened or because something is not as good as you hoped • *I was disappointed that John was not there.*

ID card /aɪ diː kɑːˈd/ **(ID cards)** NOUN An **ID card** is a card with information about a person on it. • *Don't leave bank or ID cards lying around.*

invention /ɪnˈvenʃən/ **(inventions)** NOUN something that someone has thought of or made for the first time • *Paper was a Chinese invention.*

inventor /ɪnˈventə/ **(inventors)** NOUN the first person to think of something or to make it • *Who was the inventor of the telephone?*

laboratory /ləˈbɒrətri/ **(laboratories)** NOUN a building or a room where scientific work is done • *He works in a research laboratory at Columbia University.*

landline /ˈlændlaɪn/ **(landlines)** NOUN a phone line that is fixed, instead of one that can be moved around • *One in five Britons no longer uses a landline.*

light bulb /laɪt bʌlb/ **(light bulbs)** NOUN the glass part that you put in an electric light to produce light • *There was a light bulb hanging from the ceiling.*

machine /məˈʃiːn/ **(machines)** NOUN a piece of equipment that uses electricity or an engine to do a particular job • *I put the coin in the coffee machine.*

monument /ˈmɒnjʊmənt/ **(monuments)** NOUN A **monument** is something such as a castle which was built a very long time ago and is seen as being an important part of a country's history. • *We visited the ancient monuments of England.*

musical /ˈmjuːzɪkəl/ **(musicals)** NOUN a play or a film that uses singing and dancing in the story • *Have you seen the musical, 'Miss Saigon'?*

mystery /ˈmɪstəri/ **(mysteries)** NOUN something that you cannot explain or understand • *Why he behaved in this way is a mystery.*

option /ˈɒpʃən/ **(options)** NOUN If you choose the **healthy option**, you choose something that is better for you than the other choices. • *Each school offers a healthy option on its daily menu.*

palace /ˈpælɪs/ **(palaces)** NOUN a very large impressive house where a king, a queen or a president lives • *We visited Buckingham Palace.*

professional /prəˈfeʃənəl/ ADJECTIVE doing a particular activity as a job rather than just for enjoyment • *My parents were professional musicians.*

sight /saɪt/ **(sights)** NOUN a place that is interesting to see and that tourists often visit • *We saw the sights of Paris.*

ski slope /skiː sloʊp/ **(ski slopes)** NOUN somewhere that you can ski down • *Dubai already has the world's first ski slope in a shopping mall.*

statue /ˈstætʃuː/ **(statues)** NOUN a large model of a person or an animal, made of stone or metal • *She gave me a stone statue of a horse.*

stone /stəʊn/ **(stones)** NOUN a piece of rock that is found on the ground • *For the garden, it is better to use a few really big stones.*

ton /tʌn/ **(tons)** NOUN a unit of weight • *Hundreds of tons of oil spilled into the sea.*

train /treɪn/ **(trains, training, trained)** VERB to learn the skills that you need in order to do something • *Stephen is training to be a teacher.*

TEST 5

achievement /əˈtʃiːvmənt/ **(achievements)** NOUN something that you have succeeded in doing, especially after a lot of effort • *Being chosen for the team was a great achievement.*

attention /əˈtenʃən/ NOUN If someone **pays attention**, they watch and listen carefully. • *Are you paying attention to what I'm saying?*

booking /ˈbʊkɪŋ/ **(bookings)** NOUN the arrangement that you make when you book something such as a hotel room or a table at a restaurant • *I suggest you tell him there was a mistake over his late booking*

cultural /ˈkʌltʃərəl/ ADJECTIVE used when you are talking about the arts • *We've organised a range of sports and cultural events.*

delighted /dɪˈlaɪtɪd/ ADJECTIVE extremely pleased • *Frank was delighted to see her.*

economic /ˌiːkəˈnɒmɪk, ˌek-/ ADJECTIVE used when talking about the organisation of the money and industry of a country • *The economic situation is very bad.*

exceptionally /ɪkˈsepʃənəli/ ADVERB to a very high degree • *He's an exceptionally talented dancer.*

get the feel of /get ðə fiːl əv/ PHRASE If you **get the feel of** something, for example a place or a new activity, you become familiar with it. • *He wanted to get the feel of the place.*

financial /faɪˈnænʃəl, fɪ-/ ADJECTIVE used when you are talking about money • *The company is in financial difficulties.*

futuristic /ˌfjuːtʃərɪstɪk/ ADJECTIVE very modern and unusual, like something from the future • *The theatre is a futuristic steel and glass building.*

historical /hɪstɒrɪkəl/ ADJECTIVE **Historical** people or things lived or happened in the past and are thought to be a part of history • *In Buda, several historical monuments can be seen.*

hopefully /ˈhəʊpfʊli/ ADVERB You say **hopefully** when talking about something that you hope will happen. • *Hopefully, you won't have any problems after reading this.*

seafood /ˈsiːfuːd/ NOUN fish and other small animals from the sea that you can eat • *Let's find a seafood restaurant.*

ski lift /skiːlɪft/ (ski lifts) NOUN A **ski lift** is a machine for taking people to the top of a slope so that they can ski down it. • *A new ski lift will open in December this year.*

strongly /strɒŋli/ ADVERB If you feel or say something **strongly**, you have opinions that you will not change easily. • *Obviously you feel very strongly about this.*

technique /tekˈniːk/ (techniques) NOUN a special way of doing something practical • *Doctors have recently developed these new techniques.*

TEST 6

in advance /ɪn ædˈvɑːns/ PHRASE If something is done **in advance**, it is done before a particular date or event. • *We bought our tickets for the show in advance.*

asphalt /æsfælt, -fɔːlt/ NOUN a black substance used to make things like roads and playgrounds • *The main runway is being replaced with asphalt.*

billion /ˈbɪljən/ (billions) NUMBER the number 1,000,000,000 • *The country's debt has risen to 3 billion dollars.*

canteen /kænˈtiːn/ (canteens) NOUN a place in a school or college where students can buy and eat lunch • *Rebecca ate her lunch in the canteen.*

church /tʃɜːtʃ/ (churches) NOUN a building where Christians go to pray • *The family has gone to church.*

crash /kræʃ/ (crashes, crashing, crashed) VERB If something **crashes** somewhere, it moves and hits something else with a loud noise. • *We watched the waves crash against the cliffs.*

dishwasher /ˈdɪʃwɒʃə/ (dishwashers) NOUN a machine that washes and dries dishes • *I've just bought a new dishwasher.*

dry cleaner's /draɪ /kliːnəʳz/ NOUN a shop where clothes are cleaned with a special chemical rather than with water • *There's a dry cleaner's on the corner of the street.*

edge /edʒ/ (edges) NOUN the part of something that is farthest from the middle • *She was standing at the water's edge.*

exact /ɪgˈzækt/ ADJECTIVE correct and complete in every way • *Can you tell me the exact date of the incident?*

firework /ˈfaɪəˌwɜːk/ (fireworks) NOUN a thing that flies up into the air and explodes, making bright colours in the sky • *We watched the fireworks from the balcony.*

giant /ˈdʒaɪənt/ ADJECTIVE very large or important • *They watched the concert on a giant TV screen.*

hike /haɪk/ (hikes, hiking, hiked) VERB to go for a long walk in the country • *We plan to hike the Samaria Gorge.*

ice rink /aɪs rɪŋk/ (ice rinks) NOUN a large area of ice where people go to ice-skate • *There were hundreds of skaters on the ice rink.*

last /lɑːst/ (lasts, lasting, lasted) VERB to continue to exist for a particular length of time • *The marriage lasted for less than two years.*

mixture /ˈmɪkstʃə/ (mixtures) NOUN a substance that you make by mixing different substances together • *The sauce is a mixture of chocolate and cream.*

palace /'pælɪs/ (**palaces**) NOUN a very large impressive house where a king, a queen or a president lives • *We visited Buckingham Palace.*

take place /teɪk pleɪs/ PHRASE If something **takes place**, it happens. • *The discussions took place in Paris.*

recycle /ˌriːˈsaɪkəl/ (**recycles, recycling, recycled**) VERB to put things such as paper or bottles that have already been used through a process so that they can be used again • *We try to recycle by setting up bins to collect used tins and bottles.*

recycled /ˌriːˈsaɪkəld/ ADJECTIVE things that have been recycled • *It was made of recycled plastic.*

roadworks /roʊdwɜːˈks/ PLURAL NOUN repairs or work being done on a road • *The roadworks will begin in March.*

rollercoaster /roʊləˈkoʊstəˈ/ (**rollercoasters**) NOUN a small railway at a fair that goes up and down steep slopes fast and that people go on for fun • *I've been on the rollercoaster five times.*

rough /rʌf/ ADJECTIVE If the sea is **rough**, the weather is windy or stormy and there are very big waves. • *A fishing boat sank in rough seas.*

seat /siːt/ (**seats, seating, seated**) VERB If someone **is seated**, they are sitting down. • *I met some people at the table where I was seated.*

ski slope /skiː sloʊp/ (**ski slopes**) NOUN somewhere that you can ski down • *Dubai already has the world's first ski slope in a shopping mall.*

smart /smɑːt/ ADJECTIVE clean and tidy • *Members must wear a smart jacket and tie in the restaurant.*

surface /'sɜːfɪs/ (**surfaces**) NOUN the flat top part or the outside of something • *There were pen marks on the table's surface.*

torch /tɔːtʃ/ (**torches**) NOUN a small electric light that you carry in your hand • *Everyone is asked to bring a torch.*

turn /tɜːn/ (**turns, turning, turned**) VERB If someone or something **turns into** something else, it becomes that other thing. • *In the story, the prince turns into a frog.*

TEST 7

appear /əˈpɪə/ (**appears, appearing, appeared**) VERB to take part in a play or show • *She appeared in several of his plays.*

early on /'ɜːli ɒn/ PHRASE If something happens **early on**, it happens near the beginning. • *I was two minutes behind early on in the race.*

emergency services /ɪmɜːˈdʒənsi sɜːˈvɪsɪz/ PLURAL NOUN the people in the fire brigade, the police and the ambulance service • *There was nothing I could do until the emergency services got there.*

expect /ɪkˈspekt/ (**expects, expecting, expected**) VERB If you **are expecting**, you have a baby growing inside you. • *She announced that she was expecting another child.*

full-time /fʊltaɪm/ ADJECTIVE for all of each normal working week • *I'm looking for a full-time job.*

give up /gɪv ʌp/ (**gives up, giving up, gave up**) PHRASAL VERB to stop doing or having something • *We gave up hope of finding the fishermen.*

jazz /dʒæz/ NOUN a style of music that has strong rhythms • *The club plays live jazz on Sundays.*

location /ləʊˈkeɪʃən/ (**locations**) NOUN the place where something is • *For dates and locations of the meetings, call this number.*

look back /lʊk bæk/ (**looks back, looking back, looked back**) PHRASAL VERB If you **look back**, you think about things that happened in the past. • *Looking back, I am amazed how easily it was all arranged.*

manage /'mænɪdʒ/ (**manages, managing, managed**) VERB to succeed in doing something, especially something difficult • *Three girls managed to escape the fire.*

notice /'nəʊtɪs/ (**notices, noticing, noticed**) VERB to become aware of someone or something • *Did you notice anything unusual about him?*

part-time /pɑːˈtaɪm/ ADJECTIVE working for only part of each day or week • *She is trying to get a part-time job in an office.*

recording /rɪˈkɔːdɪŋ/ (**recordings**) NOUN A **recording** of something is a record, CD, tape or video of it. • *The recording included 90 minutes of music from around the world.*

train /treɪn/ (**trains, training, trained**) VERB to learn the skills that you need in order to do something • *Stephen is training to be a teacher.*

wait /weɪt/ (**waits, waiting, waited**) VERB If you **can't wait to** do something, you are very excited about doing it. • *We can't wait to get started.*

wedding /'wedɪŋ/ (**weddings**) NOUN a marriage ceremony and the party that often takes place after the ceremony • *Many couples want a big wedding.*

TEST 8

absolutely /ˌæbsə'luːtli/ ADVERB totally and completely • *Joan is absolutely right.*

break down /breɪk daʊn/ (**breaks down, breaking down, broke down**) PHRASAL VERB to stop working • *Their car broke down.*

cancel /'kænsəl/ (**cancels, cancelling, cancelled**) VERB to say that something that has been planned will not happen • *We cancelled our trip to Washington.*

cause /kɔːz/ (**causes, causing, caused**) VERB to make something happen • *Stress can cause headaches.*

choice /tʃɔɪs/ (**choices**) NOUN the thing or things that you choose • *Her mother didn't really agree with her choice.*
NOUN If you have **no choice**, you are unable to choose to do something else. • *We had to agree, we had no choice.*

die out /daɪ aʊt/ (**dies out, dying out, died out**) PHRASAL VERB If something **dies out**, it becomes less and less common and then disappears. • *How did the dinosaurs die out?*

at least /ət liːst/ PHRASE **At least** is used to mean not less than a particular number or amount. • *Drink at least half a pint of milk each day.*

link /lɪŋk/ (**links**) NOUN a connection between two things, often because one of them causes the other • *Scientists believe there is a link between poor diet and cancer.*

news /njuːz/ NOUN information about recent events that is reported in newspapers, or on the radio, television or internet • *Here are some of the top stories in the news.*

until further notice /ʌn'tɪl 'fɜːðə 'nəʊtɪs/ PHRASE If something is happening **until further notice**, it will go on until someone changes it. • *All flights had been cancelled until further notice.*

pickpocket /pɪkpɒkɪt/ (**pickpockets**) NOUN a person who steals things from people's pockets or bags • *They knew that pickpockets were known to work in the station.*

take place /teɪk pleɪs/ PHRASE If something **takes place**, it happens. • *The discussions took place in Paris.*

possibility /ˌpɒsɪ'bɪlɪti/ (**possibilities**) NOUN a situation when something might happen • *There is a possibility that they jailed the wrong man.*

shelter /'ʃeltə/ NOUN protection from bad weather or danger • *They took shelter under a tree.*

surprising /sə'praɪzɪŋ/ ADJECTIVE not expected and making you feel surprised • *It is not surprising that children learn to read at different rates.*

training /treɪnɪŋ/ NOUN preparation for a sports competition • *He keeps fit through exercise and training.*

turn /tɜːn/ (**turns, turning, turned**) VERB If you **turn to** a job, or way of doing something, you start doing or using it. • *In the winter, they turned to fishing.*

vegetarian /ˌvedʒɪ'teəriən/ (**vegetarians**) NOUN someone who never eats meat or fish • *When did you decide to become a vegetarian?*

Audio scripts

These are the audio scripts for the Listening and Speaking papers of the tests. Listen to the audio online at: www.collinselt.com/audio

TEST 1   LISTENING

Part 1

Track 01

Key English Test, Listening.
There are five parts to the test. You will hear each piece twice.
We will now stop for a moment.
Please ask any questions now, because you must not speak during the test.
Now look at the instructions for Part 1.
For each question, choose the correct answer.
Look at Question 1.

1   *How will David travel?*

Woman:	Hi David. What a lot of luggage! Where are you going?
Man:	I'm going on holiday.
Woman:	Are you going to the airport?
Man:	Well, we wanted to fly, but the flights were so expensive.
Woman:	Hmm. The train can be too.
Man:	But we found discount train tickets online. Even cheaper than the coach.
Woman:	Have a good trip!

Now listen again.

2   *What time will Roger see the dentist?*

Roger:	Hello. Can I make an appointment to see the dentist, please?
Receptionist:	Let me see ... There are times available next Friday. How about one o'clock?
Roger:	I've got a working lunch then. Is there anything later? I can come after 3.00.
Receptionist:	I've got one available at three, and one at half past three.
Roger:	OK, I'll take the later one, please.

Now listen again.

3   *How much will Vera pay for her lunch?*

Vera:	Can I have my bill, please?
Man:	You had the chicken, correct? That's seven pounds fifty.
Vera:	And chocolate cake. That's three pounds, isn't it? So that's ... ten pounds fifty pence.
Man:	Today dessert is half price. So seven pounds fifty pence plus one pound fifty.
Vera:	So nine. Here's a ten-pound note.
Man:	I'll get your change.

Now listen again.

4   *What will the friends do in the afternoon?*

Man:	Would you like to play tennis this afternoon?
Woman:	Maybe. I was thinking of going to the indoor swimming pool.
Man:	But the weather's lovely!
Woman:	What about the beach?
Man:	But we can't play tennis on the beach.
Woman:	They say the weather will change, so let's go to the beach before it's too late.
Man:	OK, we'll keep tennis and the pool for another day.

Now listen again.

5   *What pet will Janet have?*

Mum:	Janet wants a dog.
Dad:	Not in this house. A cat, possibly, or a fish.
Mum:	She can't play with a fish. That's why she wants a dog.
Dad:	We can go on holiday and leave a fish alone.
Mum:	You can leave cats too. I say a cat.
Dad:	Fine. I still think a fish would be good. Just don't ask me to look after the cat!

Now listen again.

That is the end of Part 1.

Part 2

Track 02

Now look at Part 2.
For each question, write the correct answer in the gap.
Write one word or a number or a date or a time. Look at questions 6–10 now.
You have ten seconds.
You will hear a woman talking to a group of students about the library.

Woman:	Welcome to the library. You will all come here a lot, so there's some important information that you need to know. First of all, the hours the library is open. During term time, the library is open 24 hours a day. But outside term time, it's open from half past eight in the morning until seven o'clock in the evening. Of course, you will want to take things out of the library. You can borrow different things, like magazines, CDs, books. You can take up to ten different things out of the library, but only six books at one time. But please be careful! If you return things late, you will have to pay a fine! The cost is two pounds a day for each book and one pound a day for other things.

Library cards are free, but you need to fill in a form and give it in with a photo. If you lose your card, you can get a new one, but it will cost five pounds.

Now listen again.

That is the end of Part 2.

Part 3

Track 03

Now look at Part 3.

For each question, choose the correct answer. Look at questions 11–15 now. You have twenty seconds.
You will hear Jane talking to her friend, David, about going to the cinema.

Jane:	Hi David. Have you got any plans for this evening? Some of us are thinking of going to the cinema.
David:	Hello Jane. That sounds great. What are you going to see?
Jane:	Well, we haven't decided yet. There's a new action film out – a James Bond film. But Robert's coming and he isn't a fan of action films.
David:	What else is on?
Jane:	Let me try and remember what I saw on the website. There was a romantic film – two people fall in love, but one of them gets ill and dies young. It sounds good, but really sad.
David:	No ... I really don't enjoy films like that at all. Are there any other choices?
Jane:	There's a comedy, and people say it's very funny. And a cartoon for children.
David:	Well what about the funny one? Everyone likes a laugh, don't they?
Jane:	OK, yeah, why not? Shall we pick you up on our way there? About eight?
David:	That's a plan!

Now listen again.

That is the end of Part 3.

Part 4

Track 04

Now look at Part 4.
For each question, choose the correct answer.

16 *You will hear a woman talking to her friend about a meal at a restaurant. What did she eat?*

Man:	Did you enjoy your meal last night?
Woman:	It was delicious.
Man:	What did you have?
Woman:	Well, it was a steak restaurant, but there were other things on the menu, too, like fish and pasta.
Man:	David told me he had the pasta.
Woman:	Yes, but then he spent the whole meal looking at my fish!

Now listen again.

17 *You will hear a man explaining why he was late for work. Why was he late?*

Man:	I'm sorry for being late. I couldn't do anything about it. I woke up earlier than usual and got my train OK. And the train was on time today for a change. But the road from the station was blocked with traffic, so the bus took over an hour – usually it's a ten-minute journey. The traffic lights weren't working.

Now listen again.

18 *You will hear two friends talking about holidays. Where did Anita go?*

Man:	Did you have a nice holiday, Anita?
Anita:	Fantastic, thanks.
Man:	You went to New York, didn't you?
Anita:	We did. Not that it was planned!
Man:	Oh.
Anita:	You see, we had booked Florida, but we were offered a change at the last moment because of the bad weather there. Los Angeles was also a possibility.
Man:	Nice to have a choice!

Now listen again.

19 *You will hear two friends talking about shopping. What do they need from the supermarket?*

Woman:	Please get some potatoes when you go out.
Man:	We've got some. They're in the cupboard with the other vegetables.
Woman:	Oh. But there aren't any carrots.
Man:	Because we never eat them. We buy them and then we throw them out.
Woman:	But I want to make carrot cake. I haven't made it for months.
Man:	OK. Onions?
Woman:	We're OK for onions.

Now listen again.

20 *You will hear a man talking on the phone. Why can't he come to the party?*

Man:	I'm sorry. I left work early so I could come, but it's my mother. You met her when she visited me, didn't you? She's had a fall and I want to check that she's all right. I need to pay her a visit, anyway. I was going to see her tomorrow after work, but I think I should go now.

Now listen again.

That is the end of Part 4.

Part 5

Track 05

Now look at Part 5.
For each question, choose the correct answer.
Look at Questions 21 to 25 now.
You have 15 seconds.

You will hear Greta talking to Anthony about holidays. What type of holiday will each person go on?

Greta:	Hello Anthony. Are you getting ready for your holiday?
Anthony:	Yes, Greta. We're very excited. We've got new boots this year and we're going to try and do about 16 kilometres a day!
Greta:	Great.
Anthony:	I talked to Julie earlier. She's got her suncream and hat ready – it's sun, sea and sand for her holiday this year.
Greta:	Yes, and she said I could use her tent. My sister and I are going to Scotland.
Anthony:	Sleeping out in a field? That's not for me. I hope the weather is nice for you.
Greta:	Talking about holidays, you know John, my neighbour?
Anthony:	Yes. Didn't he go skiing last winter?
Greta:	Yes, and he broke his leg. He said 'never again!' after that. He's booked a tour of four European capital cities – he showed me a long list of interesting places he's going to visit.
Anthony:	I thought he was going cycling with Jenny.
Greta:	That was the plan, but not anymore. Jenny couldn't go. She has to work all summer.
Anthony:	She'll be home alone, then because Ed will be away on his boat.

Now listen again.

That is the end of Part 5. You now have six minutes to write your answers on the answer sheet.

That is the end of the test.

TEST 1 SPEAKING

Part 1

Track 06

Examiner:	Good morning. Can I have your mark sheets, please? I'm Adam Brown. And this is Kate Mann. Candidate A, what's your name, please?
Candidate A:	My name's Melody Karra.
Examiner:	And Candidate B, what's your name, please?
[PAUSE FOR YOU TO ANSWER]	
Examiner:	Candidate B, do you work or are you a student?
[PAUSE FOR YOU TO ANSWER]	
Examiner:	Where do you live, Candidate B?
[PAUSE FOR YOU TO ANSWER]	
Examiner:	Thank you.
Candidate A,	Do you work or are you a student?

Candidate A:	I'm a student, too.
Examiner:	Where do you live?
Candidate A:	I live in Koukaki, in Athens.
Examiner:	Thank you.
Examiner:	Now, let's talk about family. Candidate A, when do you spend time with your family?
Candidate A:	I spend time with my family on Sundays. It's the day when we have a big meal together.
Examiner:	What do you like doing with your family?
Candidate A:	I like sitting around the table with my family and eating with them. And afterwards we often go for a walk.
Examiner:	Candidate B, who are your family members?
[PAUSE FOR YOU TO ANSWER]	
Examiner:	How much time do you spend with your family?
[PAUSE FOR YOU TO ANSWER]	
Examiner:	Now Candidate A, please tell me something about one person in your family.
Candidate A:	My sister is five years younger than me. She's always very happy and everyone loves her. She likes singing and dancing.
Examiner:	Now, let's talk about sport. Candidate B, how much sport do you play?
[PAUSE FOR YOU TO ANSWER]	
Examiner:	Who do you play sport with, Candidate B?
[PAUSE FOR YOU TO ANSWER]	
Examiner:	Candidate A, what sports are you good at?
Candidate A:	I'm not very good at them, but I like badminton.
Examiner:	When do you play sport?
Candidate A:	I don't play it very often, but when we go to the beach, I play badminton with my sister.
Examiner:	Now Candidate B, please tell me about your favourite sport.
[PAUSE FOR YOU TO ANSWER]	
Examiner:	Thank you.

Part 2

Track 07

Examiner:	Now, in this part of the test you are going to talk together. Here are some pictures that show different ways of travelling. Do you like these different ways of travelling? Say why or why not. I'll say that again.

Do you like these different ways of travelling? Say why or why not. All right? Now, talk together.

Candidate A: I think driving a car is a good way to travel. You can leave when you want to and go exactly where you want to. What do you think?

[PAUSE FOR YOU TO ANSWER]

Candidate A: What do you think about travelling by train?

[PAUSE FOR YOU TO ANSWER]

Candidate A: I use the bus a lot in Athens. It's easy to catch the bus. I have a travel card so I don't have to pay every time.

[PAUSE FOR YOU TO ANSWER]

Candidate A: I don't think cycling is a very good idea in a big city. It can be dangerous when there's a lot of traffic. What do you think?

[PAUSE FOR YOU TO ANSWER]

Candidate A: Walking is a good way to travel if you don't have a long way to go. If the weather is fine, it can be nice. How do you feel about walking?

[PAUSE FOR YOU TO ANSWER]

Examiner: Candidate A, do you think cars are a cheap way to travel?

Candidate A: No, I don't.

Examiner: Why, Candidate B?

Candidate A: You have to buy a car, and a good car is expensive. You have to put petrol in it and petrol isn't cheap. You also need to repair it sometimes.

Examiner: Candidate B, do you think cycling is fun?

[PAUSE FOR YOU TO ANSWER]

Examiner: So Candidate A, which of these ways of travelling do you like the most?

Candidate A: I like travelling by car the most.

Examiner: And you, Candidate B, which of these ways of travelling do you like the least?

[PAUSE FOR YOU TO ANSWER]

Examiner: Thank you.

Examiner: Now, would you prefer to walk or cycle, Candidate B?

[PAUSE FOR YOU TO ANSWER]

Examiner: Why?

[PAUSE FOR YOU TO ANSWER]

Examiner: And what about you, Candidate A? Would you prefer to travel by bus or by train?

Candidate A: If I am going a long way, I prefer to travel by train. I think a train is more comfortable and you have more room on a train.

Examiner: Do you think cars are safe, Candidate A?

Candidate A: Yes, I do.

Examiner: Why?

Candidate A: If you are a careful driver, then a car is safe.

Examiner: Do you think cars are safe, Candidate B?

[PAUSE FOR YOU TO ANSWER]

Examiner: Thank you. That is the end of the test.

TEST 2   LISTENING

Part 1

Track 08

Key English Test, Listening
There are five parts to the test. You will hear each piece twice.
We will now stop for a moment.
Please ask any questions now, because you must not speak during the test.
Now look at the instructions for Part 1.
For each question, choose the correct answer.
Look at Question 1.

1 *What might Mark look like now?*

Woman: Are you excited to see Mark? When was the last time you saw him?

Man: Four years ago, when he came here as an exchange student.

Woman: He must look different now. Is he still short with short blond hair?

Man: I don't think so – he told me he's grown it, and he'll definitely be taller now!

Now listen again.

2 *What will the woman probably study next year?*

Man: Are you going to continue studying geography next year?

Woman: Well, it isn't a main subject so I don't have to. I never really enjoyed it, so I'd prefer to do something else. Maths might be more useful if I study business at university. How about you?

Man: I'm not sure either, but I think I want to continue with history.

Now listen again.

3 *What is David making for dinner?*

Tina: What are you doing, David?

David: Oh, hi, Tina. I've just made dinner. It'll be the last time we eat together before we go home for the holidays. I hope you like burgers and chips.

Tina: Yes! It's my favourite. I can make the salad if you like.

David: Thanks! And if Brian joins us, I'll make an omelette – he doesn't eat meat.

Now listen again.

4 *What time does the exam begin?*

Woman: I'm really worried about the exam, Max.

Max: Me, too. I was up all night studying. I can't wait until three o'clock when it will be over.

Woman: Well, it's only a half-hour speaking exam. I'm going to get there early, around two o'clock so I can relax before it begins.

Max: Good idea. I'll come with you.

Now listen again.

5 *Where does the woman think she lost her purse?*

Man: Did you find your purse?

Woman: No, unfortunately, and I had £20 in it and my college ID card.

Man: Where do you think you lost it?

Woman: I had it at the library – I remember because I paid for a late book. Then I paid for tickets at the cinema. But it wasn't in my bag when I tried to pay for milk at the supermarket.

Now listen again.

That is the end of Part 1.

Part 2

Track 09

Now look at Part 2.
For each question, write the correct answer in the gap.
Write one word or a number or a date or a time. Look at questions 6–10 now.
You have ten seconds.
You will hear a woman talking about her work experience.

Jessica: My name's Jessica Chapman and I'd like to tell you about a job I did a few months ago. I worked as an online language teacher. I helped schoolchildren in China to learn English. I talked to them online using special software for two hours every Monday and Wednesday. My students were all young, eight to ten years old and about the same level. The groups I taught were small: three to six students in each lesson.
I had an interactive whiteboard on my screen that I could write and draw on. The students could see it on their screens, too. We played games, sang songs and had conversations.
I saw an advert for the job in January, and I applied immediately. A month later I got a reply, and I started working in July. I want to be a teacher in the future and this job gave me lots of experience. I really loved it, and I was sad when the job came to an end in September.

Now listen again.

That is the end of Part 2.

Part 3

Track 10

Now look at Part 3.
For each question, choose the correct answer. Look at questions 11–15 now. You have 20 seconds.
You will hear Laura talking to her friend John about her trip to Scotland.

John: How was Scotland, Laura? Did you visit any universities?

Laura: Yes, in Aberdeen, Dundee and St Andrews. The last one was in Edinburgh. We wanted to visit Glasgow, too, but there wasn't enough time.

John: Did you go alone?

Laura: No. I was going to go with my mum but my dad and brother came, too.

John: Where did you stay?

Laura: The hotels were either full or too expensive. Then we learned that visitors can rent rooms in the universities. They were even cheaper than a guest house!

John: What did you think of the universities?

Laura: Well, most universities are in large cities and they all have interesting courses. But I preferred St Andrews because it's by the sea and the countryside around it is beautiful. It's one of the oldest universities in the world and Mum loved the buildings.

John: What about Edinburgh?

Laura: It's a great city with lots of shops, cafés and museums, but it's expensive to live there as a student.

John: So have you decided where you want to go?

Laura: Not yet.

Now listen again.

That is the end of Part 3.

Part 4

Track 11

Now look at Part 4.
For each question, choose the correct answer.

16 *You will hear a teacher talking to a student. What does he say about her work?*

Mr Davies: Rosie, can I speak to you about your project?

Rosie: Oh no, Mr Davies! Was it very bad?

Mr Davies: No, not at all, it was good, better than your last project, but it could be even better. The homework you gave me yesterday was excellent, so I want your next project to be as good as your homework.

Rosie: All right, I'll try.

Now listen again.

17 *You will hear a man talking to his friend about a photograph. Who is the woman in the photograph?*

Woman: So, who's that woman in the photo?
Man: That's Clara. She's my father's youngest sister, my aunt.
Woman: She's very young!
Man: Yes, she she's only ten years older than me. People usually think she's my cousin.
Woman: How old was your dad when she was born?
Man: Sixteen, so really, she's more like a sister to me than to him.

Now listen again.

18 *You will hear a man talking to his friend about a jacket. Why did he buy it?*

Woman: Hi Peter. Did you go shopping today?
Peter: Yes, and I bought a jacket.
Woman: Another one?! Can I see it?
Peter: Yes, look. It's for football practice during the winter.
Woman: Oh, it's great! You could wear it every day, too. Sports clothes are in fashion now.
Peter: Yes, I could, but I have to dress more smartly when I'm at work.

Now listen again.

19 *You will hear a mother talking to her son. Why is she unhappy?*

Woman: Where have you been, Karl?
Karl: I went to the supermarket for some milk. Dad asked me to get some this morning.
Woman: OK, but next time take your boots off when you come in. Look at the floor! I'll need to clean it again!
Karl: Oh, sorry, Mum!

Now listen again.

20 *You will hear two friends talking about their day. What did they do first?*

Woman: What a busy day! I'm so tired! It was fun, though, and it's nice to end the day here.
Man: I enjoyed it, too. The museum was really interesting.
Woman: Yes, it was, but I'm glad we went there before going shopping.
Man: And now I want something to eat. I'm hungry!

Now listen again.

That is the end of Part 4.

Part 5

Track 12

Now look at Part 5.
For each question, choose the correct answer.
Look at Questions 21 to 25 now.
You have 15 seconds.

You will hear Sally talking to James about different documents and books. Which person do they belong to?

Sally: What are you doing, James?
James: Hey, Sally. I'm looking through these old documents before I throw them away. They've been in this cupboard for years.
Sally: I'll help you. ... Oh look! This is Dad's. Remember that year when we arrived at the airport and he couldn't find it because he'd left it at home?
James: *(laughs)* Yes, and we nearly missed our flight. ... Is that an old notebook?
Sally: No... Oh, it's full of Jane's writing. It's her diary, the one she had years ago. She wanted to write in it – her feelings, the things that happened every day. But in the end, she just wrote what she had for dinner!
James: Well, she's always been interested in food, like Mum.
Sally: And talking of Mum, look at this!
James: It's from that old restaurant ... *(remembering name)* La Strada. She and Dad went there a lot before it closed. I guess she kept it as a souvenir. And hey! Look at this old photo of Granny!
Sally: Why is her licence *here*?
James: Well, she hasn't got a car anymore. Anyway, it's very, very old.
Sally: Let's keep it. I want the photo for my photo album.
James: What's in that envelope next to the box with the postcards?
Sally: Er ... let's see ... it's old bills for electricity and water and things like that.
James: They're Grandpa's. He never throws *anything* away.
Sally: And that? Another diary?
James: I don't think so. It says 'George Barron' on the cover, and this is George's writing: 'French Vocabulary'! He wasn't very good at French, was he?

Now listen again.
That is the end of Part 5. You now have six minutes to write your answers on the answer sheet.
That is the end of the test.

TEST 2   SPEAKING

Part 1

Track 13

Examiner: Good afternoon.
Can I have your mark sheets, please?
I'm Hannah Jones. And this is Keith Mantell.
What's your name, Candidate A?
Candidate A: My name's Andrea Chiti.
Examiner: And what's your name, Candidate B?

[PAUSE FOR YOU TO ANSWER]

Examiner: Candidate B, do you work or are you a student?

[PAUSE FOR YOU TO ANSWER]

Examiner: Where do you come from, Candidate B?

[PAUSE FOR YOU TO ANSWER]

Examiner: Thank you.
Candidate A, do you work or are you a student?

Candidate A: I'm a student, too.

Examiner: Where do you come from?

Candidate A: I come from Rome in Italy.

Examiner: Thank you.

Examiner: Now, let's talk about jobs.
Candidate A, what job would you like to have?

Candidate A: I'm studying medicine at university, and one day I want to work as a doctor in a big hospital.

Examiner: Why do you want to be a doctor?

Candidate A: Because I think medicine is the most interesting subject to study, and I also want to help people.

Examiner: Candidate B, what kinds of jobs do you think young people want to do?

[PAUSE FOR YOU TO ANSWER]

Examiner: Would you like to work in an office, Candidate B?

[PAUSE FOR YOU TO ANSWER]

Examiner: Now Candidate A, please tell me something about a job that you wouldn't like to do.

Candidate A: I wouldn't like to have a job in an office or a factory. I think it would be very boring, and a job in a factory is also very hard.

Examiner: Now, let's talk about friends.
Candidate B, how often do you see your friends?

[PAUSE FOR YOU TO ANSWER]

Examiner: And Candidate B, what do you like doing with your friends?

[PAUSE FOR YOU TO ANSWER]

Examiner: Candidate A, where do your friends live?

Candidate A: Most of my friends live in the same part of Rome as me and a few live in the countryside outside the city.

Examiner: When do you see your friends?

Candidate A: I usually don't get a chance to see my friends during the week, so I usually see them on Saturday or Sunday.

Examiner: Now Candidate B, please tell me something about one of your friends.

[PAUSE FOR YOU TO ANSWER]

Part 2

Track 14

Examiner: Now, in this part of the test you are going to talk together.
Here are some pictures that show different places to live.
Do you like these different places to live? Say why or why not. I'll say that again.
Do you like these different places to live? Say why or why not.
All right? Now, talk together.

Candidate A: I think it's nice to live in the apartment building and the house. How about you?

[PAUSE FOR YOU TO ANSWER]

Candidate A: Why do you like houseboats?

[PAUSE FOR YOU TO ANSWER]

Candidate A: Well, I couldn't live on a farm or in a quiet village. In an apartment building, if you live at the top, you have great views!

Examiner: Candidate A, why do you think living in a house is nice?

Candidate A: Because houses usually have a garden and it's nice to have some outside space where you live.

Examiner: Candidate B, do you think living on a farm is fun?

[PAUSE FOR YOU TO ANSWER]

Examiner: So Candidate A, which of these places to live do you like best?

Candidate A: Well, if I have to choose between an apartment building and a house, I will choose the apartment building because they are usually in the centre of a town or city, so there are lots of shops, restaurants and interesting places to visit nearby.

Examiner: And you, Candidate B, which of these places to live do you like best?

[PAUSE FOR YOU TO ANSWER]

Examiner: Thank you.

Examiner: Now, do you prefer living in a big home or a small home, Candidate B?

[PAUSE FOR YOU TO ANSWER]

Examiner: Why, Candidate B?

[PAUSE FOR YOU TO ANSWER]

Examiner: And what about you, Candidate A? Do you prefer living in a big or small home?

Candidate A: I prefer a big home.

Examiner: Do you prefer living in cities or in the countryside, Candidate A?

Candidate A: I prefer living in cities because you have all the facilities you need, like shops, cafes, cinemas and parks.

Examiner: And you, Candidate B? Do you prefer living in cities or in the countryside?

[PAUSE FOR YOU TO ANSWER]

Examiner: Why is that, Candidate B?

[PAUSE FOR YOU TO ANSWER]

Examiner: Thank you. That is the end of the test.

TEST 3   LISTENING

Part 1

Track 15

Key English Test, Listening
There are five parts to the test. You will hear each piece twice.
We will now stop for a moment.
Please ask any questions now, because you must not speak during the test.
Now look at the instructions for Part 1.
For each question, choose the correct answer.
Look at Question 1.

1 *What time is Margaret's train?*

Man: Hi Margaret. What time's your train? The eight o'clock one?

Margaret: I wish it was! That one was full.

Man: But there isn't another one until nine fifteen. Isn't that too late?

Margaret: Yes. They've put on an extra train at quarter to nine because of the holiday, and I'm getting that.

Man: So there's one before nine fifteen.

Margaret: Yes.

Now listen again.

2 *What will Mary bring to the party?*

Man: Hi Mary. What are you bringing to the party?

Mary: I thought I'd bring some pizza.

Man: Isn't Henry bringing pizza?

Mary: No, he's bringing cake. And I hope it's a chocolate cake!

Man: Who's bringing the balloons?

Mary: Balloons? That's your job. Didn't you read the email?

Man: No, my computer is broken. OK, so I'm bringing balloons.

Now listen again.

3 *What will Roberta do this afternoon?*

Man: Hey, Roberta, please don't forget to buy sugar when you go shopping.

Roberta: I haven't got time to go shopping today.

Man: But you always go on Fridays. And these books need to go back to the library.

Roberta: I'm having my hair cut and it's going to take hours. You'll have to go to the supermarket and the library.

Now listen again.

4 *What will the friends eat for dinner?*

Man: What about dinner?

Woman: How about going out for fish and chips?

Man: Great idea, but have we got time? The film starts at eight. Maybe we should just have a sandwich?

Woman: Or soup? There's some in the fridge from yesterday.

Man: There isn't enough for two. Look, it'll only take a minute to get the bread and cheese out. Then we won't miss the film.

Woman: OK.

Now listen again.

5 *What job does Kevin's son have?*

Woman: How's the family, Kevin?

Kevin: Very well. Adam, my son, has a new job.

Woman: Oh, he's not a cook anymore?

Kevin: Well, actually, he is. He went for a job as a shop assistant at the supermarket, but they also needed cooks for the hot food they sell.

Woman: Doesn't your wife work at the supermarket, too?

Kevin: Yes, but she's in the office.

Now listen again.

That is the end of Part 1.

Part 2

Track 16

Now look at Part 2.
For each question, write the correct answer in the gap. Write one word or a number or a date or a time. Look at questions 6–10 now.
You have ten seconds.
You will hear a speaker giving information to students about staying in university flats.

Woman: Now I'm going to give you some information about university flats. The first type is the cheapest. There are ten students in each flat. A room costs £95 per week. Each term is a different number of weeks. The first term is longer than the others. It's 13 weeks, so it's more expensive: one thousand two hundred and thirty-five pounds. The second term costs nine hundred and fifty pounds, and the final term costs one thousand and forty-five pounds. The second type of flat is £110 a week and you share with three other students. In the first term, flats are available from the fifteenth of September until the twentieth of December. You can't stay in the flats during the university holidays, but you can move back in on the fourth of January for the second term. We have quiet time at night in student flats from Monday to Thursday between ten o'clock at night and half past six in the morning so students can study and sleep.

Now listen again.
That is the end of Part 2.

Part 3

Track 17

Now look at Part 3.
For each question, choose the correct answer. Look at questions 11–15 now. You have twenty seconds.
You will hear Peter talking to his friend Linda about going camping.

Linda: So, Peter, who are you going camping with?
Peter: Well, Dave from work can't make it, so Tom, Mike and Jon – you know them, old school friends. I'll do a trip with colleagues another time.
Linda: How long are you going for?
Peter: It was going to be three nights – Thursday, Friday, Saturday, but now Jon and Mike have to be back by Saturday afternoon. It's not a bad thing because I also want to do some things around the house. I really need to do some cleaning, and I'm thinking of painting the bathroom.
Linda: Oh. You're not all in one tent, are you?
Peter: It's a four-man tent with two sleeping sections, and each is big enough for two people.
Linda: What are you doing for food?
Peter: We don't want to spend all our time cooking, and we don't want to take lots of food. So we're planning to eat in cafés and restaurants. We'll take some milk and cereal with us for breakfast. That way we don't have to pay for three meals a day.

Now listen again.
That is the end of Part 3.

Part 4

Track 18

Now look at Part 4.
For each question, choose the correct answer.

16 *You will hear a woman shopping for shoes. Which pair of shoes does she buy?*

Woman: Have you got these brown shoes in size 7?
Man: Only in 6 ½ and 7 ½, I'm afraid. These green ones are similar and we've got them in all sizes.
Woman: What about these black ones?
Man: We've got those in all sizes, too.

Woman: Black it is. Green shoes don't go with my clothes and the brown ones aren't the right size.

Now listen again.

17 *You will hear a woman describing something she lost. What did she lose?*

Man: Can you describe it, please?
Woman: It's brown leather. New, expensive!
Man: What was in it?
Woman: I had my purse in my coat pocket, so no money luckily.
Man: What about keys?
Woman: Yes! Keys! I can't open my suitcase because the keys are in my handbag.
Man: Anything else?
Woman: My mobile phone. My passport is in the suitcase, so it's OK.

Now listen again.

18 *You will hear two friends talking. What is Paul going to make?*

Woman: Are you making a cake for the party, Paul?
Paul: I've already made it! I'm just having a quick lunch.
Woman: Oh. That sounds like a good idea. Anything for me?
Paul: I thought you didn't like omelettes!
Woman: Why not fry the eggs?
Paul: I've mixed them up already!

Now listen again.

19 *You will hear a man talking about his holiday to his friend. What animal did he ride?*

Woman: What was it like?
Man: Fantastic! You're high up, so it's scary!
Woman: Are they friendly?
Man: Not really, and they smell! But they're so strong.
Woman: They have to be – to live in those hot dry places.
Man: I've been on an elephant before, but it wasn't as difficult as the camel.
Woman: I think I'll keep to horses!

Now listen again.

20 *You will hear a woman talking to her friend. Why is she upset?*

Woman: ...Then the car wouldn't start, so I called a taxi to Jean's house. And it was late at night.
Man: Oh no! Of course you're upset. And you went all that way! I'm sure it was very expensive!
Woman: I've been having problems with my car, so I wasn't surprised. The taxi driver was helpful with my luggage, but Jean was out and I had to wait in the rain!

Now listen again.
That is the end of Part 4.

Part 5

Track 19

Now look at Part 5.
For each question, choose the correct answer.
Look at Questions 21 to 25 now.
You have 15 seconds.
You will hear John and Fiona talking about what to do with the family at the activity centre. What activity will each person do?

Fiona:	Let's all go to the activity centre, John. There'll be something to do for everyone.
John:	Good idea, Fiona. They've got golf for me, and there's a pool. That'll keep Billy happy. What about you? There's tennis.
Fiona:	My leg still isn't right. I think tennis is a bit much for me, but Fred wants to try it again. He didn't like badminton the first time he tried that. I'll take some time out and just watch him – give him some advice.
John:	Keith will definitely want to try out his new boots to see if they can help him score more goals. What do you think Shona will want to do? Table tennis?
Fiona:	Er, she got upset when she lost her bat. So maybe not. Swimming with Billy?
John:	I think they need a break from each other. What about badminton with those other children?
Fiona:	That will probably be all right. She always wants to do something different from everybody else. But horse-riding is out! Do you remember what happened the last time?

Now listen again.
That is the end of Part 5. You now have six minutes to write your answers on the answer sheet.
That is the end of the test.

TEST 3   SPEAKING

Part 1

Track 20

Examiner:	Good morning. Can I have your mark sheets, please? I'm Keith Mantell. And this is Hannah Jones. Candidate A, what's your name, please?
Candidate A:	My name's Jakub Nowak.
Examiner:	And Candidate B, what's your name, please?
[PAUSE FOR YOU TO ANSWER]	
Examiner:	Candidate B, do you work or are you a student?
[PAUSE FOR YOU TO ANSWER]	
Examiner:	Where do you live, Candidate B?
[PAUSE FOR YOU TO ANSWER]	
Examiner:	Thank you. Candidate A, do you work or are you a student?
Candidate A:	I'm a student.
Examiner:	Where do you come from?
Candidate A:	I come from Poznan, in Poland
Examiner:	Thank you.
Examiner:	Now, let's talk about holidays. Candidate A, how often do you go on holiday?
Candidate A:	I usually go on holiday once a year. We have a family holiday in the summer.
Examiner:	Where do you go on holiday?
Candidate A:	We often go to visit my grandparents. They live by the sea.
Examiner:	Candidate B, what kind of holidays do you like?
[PAUSE FOR YOU TO ANSWER]	
Examiner:	When do you take your holiday, Candidate B?
[PAUSE FOR YOU TO ANSWER]	
Examiner:	Now Candidate A, please tell me about a dream holiday you would like to take.
Candidate A:	I'd love to visit Florida for a holiday and see the Everglades. I'd also like to spend some time in Miami. I think it's an exciting place to visit. And of course, I'd also go to Disney World.
Examiner:	Now, let's talk about television. Candidate B, how often do you watch television?
[PAUSE FOR YOU TO ANSWER]	
Examiner:	What type of television programmes do you like, Candidate B?
[PAUSE FOR YOU TO ANSWER]	
Examiner:	Candidate A, when do you watch television?
Candidate A:	I usually watch television in the evening when I want to relax. I like watching football, so if there's a big game on then I'll definitely watch television.
Examiner:	Who do you watch television with?
Candidate A:	If I watch late at night to relax, I watch it on my own, but when I watch football matches, I watch it with my friends.
Examiner:	Now Candidate B, please tell me about the sort of television programmes that you don't like.
[PAUSE FOR YOU TO ANSWER]	
Examiner:	Thank you.

Part 2

Track 21

Examiner:	Now, in this part of the test you are going to talk together. Here are some pictures that show different pets. Do you like these different pets? Say why or why not. I'll say that again. Do you like these different pets? Say why or why not. All right? Now, talk together.
Candidate A:	I think that a dog is a very good pet. What do you think?

[PAUSE FOR YOU TO ANSWER]

Candidate A	What do you think about having a cat?

[PAUSE FOR YOU TO ANSWER]

Candidate A	I think fish are beautiful, especially colourful tropical fish, and watching them is relaxing.

[PAUSE FOR YOU TO ANSWER]

Candidate A:	I'm scared of snakes, so I don't think a snake is a good pet.

[PAUSE FOR YOU TO ANSWER]

Candidate A:	I don't think a bird is a good pet, either. I think it's cruel to keep birds in a cage. Do you like birds as pets?

[PAUSE FOR YOU TO ANSWER]

Examiner:	Candidate A, do you think having a dog is fun?
Candidate A:	Yes, I do.
Examiner:	Why?
Candidate A:	You can take a dog anywhere with you. For example, you can play with it in the park or on the beach. You can throw things for it, like a ball, and you can have a lot of fun playing games with it.
Examiner:	Candidate B, do you think cats are fun?

[PAUSE FOR YOU TO ANSWER]

Examiner:	So Candidate A, which of these pets do you like the best?
Candidate A:	I like dogs the best.
Examiner:	And you, Candidate B, which of these pets do you like the best?

[PAUSE FOR YOU TO ANSWER]

Examiner:	Thank you.
Examiner:	Now, would you prefer a fish or a bird as a pet, Candidate B?

[PAUSE FOR YOU TO ANSWER]

Examiner:	Why is that, Candidate B?

[PAUSE FOR YOU TO ANSWER]

Examiner:	And what about you, Candidate A? Would you prefer a fish or a bird as a pet?
Candidate A:	I'm not sure. I think I'd prefer a fish. Some fish are beautiful, and you can spend hours watching them. And I think they are easier to look after than birds.
Examiner:	Do you think pets are good for children, Candidate A?
Candidate A:	Yes, I do.
Examiner:	Why?
Candidate A:	Children can learn a lot from pets. They learn to look after them and they learn to be responsible.
Examiner:	Do you think pets are good for children, Candidate B?

[PAUSE FOR YOU TO ANSWER]

Examiner:	Thank you. That is the end of the test.

TEST 4   LISTENING

Part 1

Track 22

Key English Test, Listening
There are five parts to the test. You will hear each piece twice.
We will now stop for a moment.
Please ask any questions now, because you must not speak during the test.
Now look at the instructions for Part 1.
For each question, choose the correct answer.
Look at Question 1.

1   *Who is Jenny's brother?*

Man:	I hear your brother got the job, Jenny.
Jenny:	Yes. It's only part-time because he's still at school.
Man:	Let's go and order some coffee from him after basketball practice!
Jenny:	Good idea! And after that, we can go to the shoe shop on the corner. I need some smart shoes for *my* new job.

Now listen again.

2   *What will they have for dinner?*

Woman:	You aren't making sandwiches again for dinner, are you? We need to eat better than that!
Man:	I know, but I'm a terrible cook!
Woman:	Well, there's some fish in the fridge, we've got beans and potatoes ...
Man:	Oh, and here's a tin of tomato soup.
Woman:	No, I'm going to cook us a meal, and we can have the soup tomorrow.
Man:	Great.

Now listen again.

3 *Where is Carla's tent?*

Man: Have you put your tent up yet, Carla?
Carla: Yes! It's a really beautiful campsite.
Man: It is. My tent is next to Max's. We're over there, by the river so we can go fishing early in the morning.
Carla: Lucky you! I couldn't find any spaces there or under the trees, so I'm next to Emma by the lake.

Now listen again.

4   *What is Louis writing to his friend?*

Mel: You look busy, Louis. Are you writing a letter to your grandparents?
Louis: Oh, hi, Mel! No, nothing like that. I'm just writing to a friend in Singapore.
Mel: Isn't it easier to email him?
Louis: Yes, but I found this cool magazine and I know he'll like it. This is just a note to put in the envelope when I send it.

Now listen again.

5   *What did Tom forget to bring to his last exam?*

Girl: Are you ready for the exam, Tom? I hope you've remembered to bring your pen. Not like the last exam!
Tom: Don't worry. Here it is, and I've also got a ruler and a pencil. I've left my calculator in my bag.
Girl: So did I. What a pity we can't use one for this exam!

Now listen again.
That is the end of Part 1.

Part 2

Track 23

Now look at Part 2.
For each question, write the correct answer in the gap.
Write one word or a number or a date or a time. Look at questions 6–10 now.
You have ten seconds.
You will hear a student giving a presentation about Thomas Edison, the famous inventor.

Man: Thomas Alva Edison was a famous American inventor. He was born on 11th February, 1847, the seventh child of Samuel and Nancy Edison.
           Thomas wasn't a good student and he left school after only a few months. But he was interested in science and technology from an early age, and he spent hours reading scientific books and making things.
           He moved to New York City in 1869, and he soon made a lot of money from his inventions – $40,000.
           In 1871, he married Mary Stilwell, and in 1876, he opened a laboratory in a village called Menlo Park. A lot of people worked for him and helped him with

his inventions. His first great invention there was the phonograph, a machine that could record and play sound. He also invented an electric light bulb that people could use at home. His inventions made him very rich.
His wife died in 1884, but he married again in 1886. He and his second wife moved to West Orange, in New Jersey. There, Edison built another big laboratory and factories. He worked there until he died on the 18 October 1931.

Now listen again.
That is the end of Part 2.

Part 3

Track 24

Now look at Part 3.
For each question, choose the correct answer. Look at questions 11–15 now. You have twenty seconds.
You will hear Emma talking to her friend Fabio about a fashion show.

Emma: Hi Fabio. Did you go to the college fashion show last week?
Fabio: Hi, Emma! Yes, I did! Did you?
Emma: Yes, I went with some friends, but I didn't see you there. Did you go alone?
Fabio: I was going to go with a friend from college, but he was busy, so I went with my cousin Anna. She's studying fashion design at university.
Emma: When did you go? We were there on Sunday.
Fabio: We actually went twice, once on Friday afternoon and then again on Saturday for the costume show.
Emma: I missed that one. The children's fashion show was interesting, but I didn't like the sports clothes one. My friend Melissa didn't like it, either. She said it was boring.
Fabio: That was Anna's opinion, too, but I thought *all* the shows were brilliant.
Emma: There's another exhibition next month: Beautiful Plastic. I'm making some earrings and a necklace for it, but people are also making bags, shoes, even clothes. All from plastic.
Fabio: That sounds interesting. I'll be there!

Now listen again.
That is the end of Part 3.

Part 4

Track 25

Now look at Part 4.
For each question, choose the correct answer.

16   *You will hear two friends talking about an accident. What did Matt break?*

Woman: Hey, Matt! What happened to you?!

Matt:	I had a silly accident in the park. I wanted to show my little sister how to play rugby. I was running with the ball when a dog ran in front of me. I fell over him, he bit my leg, I crashed into a tree, banged my head, and broke my arm.
Woman:	How terrible!
Matt:	Actually, it was funny. As I said, it was a silly accident.

Now listen again.

17 *You will hear two people talking about some keys. Where did the man leave them?*

Woman:	Come on, Mark. We're gonna be late!
Mark:	I can't find the car keys. They aren't in the hall.
Woman:	Have you looked under the sofa? You took your coat off in here last night. Maybe they fell out of your pocket.
Mark:	I'll look now.
Woman:	Oh, don't bother. Here they are, next to the fridge. You probably put them here when you got the milk out for breakfast.

Now listen again.

18 *You will hear two friends talking in a restaurant. What does the woman decide to eat?*

Man:	I haven't been to this restaurant before. It looks nice. What are you going to have?
Woman:	I'm not sure. Maybe a salad.
Man:	I'm too hungry for a salad, but the pizzas look amazing!
Woman:	Yes, they do, and the cheeseburgers look delicious, but I think I'll go with my first idea. I'd like a glass of lemonade, too.

Now listen again.

19 *You will hear a man talking to a friend about his grandparents. What are they doing this weekend?*

Woman:	So, what are you doing this weekend?
Man:	Visiting my grandparents. They're having a party.
Woman:	That's nice. Is it someone's birthday?
Man:	No, Grandad was 72 in October. This is to meet their new neighbours. They moved to a new house last weekend.
Woman:	Did you help them move?
Man:	Yes, and my brother and sister helped too.

Now listen again.

20 *You will hear a woman talking to a friend about going to the airport. How will she get there?*

Woman:	My flight is at eight, but the first bus comes at six. It takes more than an hour, so that's too late. ... I'd love to book one, but it's expensive, and anyway, there will be a lot of traffic on the road at that hour. ... Yes, you're right. I'll ask Dad to drive me to the railway station. He won't be happy, though.

Now listen again.
That is the end of Part 4.

Part 5

Track 26

Now look at Part 5.
For each question, choose the correct answer.
Look at Questions 21 to 25 now.
You have 15 seconds.
You will hear Max talking to Ellie about a barbecue.
What will each person bring?

Max:	What time is everyone arriving for the barbecue, Ellie?
Ellie:	I told them to come around 2 p.m. I've made meat burgers, and there are vegetable burgers, too, for the vegetarians.
Max:	Good idea.
Ellie:	George is bringing ice cream and cakes. We all like to eat something sweet after lunch.
Max:	I can bring a few melons from the market. It's good to have a healthy option.
Ellie:	Thanks, Max, but you don't need to buy any fruit. Jack says he'll bring some strawberries from his mum's garden. But perhaps you can make some lemonade – with real lemons. We can put it on ice so it's nice and cold. Oh, and maybe some orange juice, too?
Max:	No problem! I'll do that. What about Sophie?
Ellie:	She said she can bring a curry or some salads. I *love* curry, but on a hot day people prefer something nice and cool!
Max:	OK, so what's Oscar bringing?
Ellie:	Nothing, but he's going to cook the burgers on the barbecue.
Max:	We should also have some sausages. Everyone loves them.
Ellie:	OK. I'll ask Oscar to bring some.

Now listen again.
That is the end of Part 5. You now have six minutes to write your answers on the answer sheet.
That is the end of the test.

TEST 4   SPEAKING

Part 1

Track 27

Examiner:	Good morning. Can I have your mark sheets, please? I'm Lucy Clarke. And this is Richard Norton. What's your name, Candidate A?
Candidate A:	My name's Ling Li.
Examiner:	And what's your name, Candidate B?
[PAUSE FOR YOU TO ANSWER]	

Examiner:	Candidate B, do you work or are you a student?

[PAUSE FOR YOU TO ANSWER]

Examiner:	Where do you come from, Candidate B?

[PAUSE FOR YOU TO ANSWER]

Examiner:	Thank you. Candidate A, do you work or are you a student?
Candidate A:	I'm a student.
Examiner:	Where do you come from?
Candidate A:	I come from Beijing in China.
Examiner:	Thank you.
Examiner:	Now, let's talk about health and exercise. Candidate A, what do you do to stay healthy?
Candidate A:	I play badminton with my friends once a week and I also walk my dog in the park every morning. I try to eat lots of healthy food, like fruit and vegetables.
Examiner:	Do you get sick often?
Candidate A:	No, I don't get sick very often, usually a couple of times a year.
Examiner:	Candidate B, how often do you exercise?

[PAUSE FOR YOU TO ANSWER]

Examiner:	When was the last time you had to go to the doctor, Candidate B?

[PAUSE FOR YOU TO ANSWER]

Examiner:	Now Candidate A, please tell me what you usually do when you don't feel well.
Candidate A:	I usually stay at home and rest. I either stay in bed or lie on the sofa and watch TV. I try to drink lots of water and my mum makes me soup.
Examiner:	Now, let's talk about technology. Candidate B, what types of technology do you use every day?

[PAUSE FOR YOU TO ANSWER]

Examiner:	What other technology is important to you in your everyday life, Candidate B?

[PAUSE FOR YOU TO ANSWER]

Examiner:	Candidate A, is there a type of technology you couldn't live without?
Candidate A:	Yes, my digital camera. I study photography at college, so I take my camera with me everywhere. I have a camera on my mobile phone, too, of course, but I don't use it for my photography work.
Examiner:	How do you prefer to search for information when you are studying?
Candidate A:	I use the internet if I want to find something quickly, but I also go

to the library and look for old photographs in books, magazines and journals.

Examiner:	Now Candidate B, please tell me if there is a time when you prefer not to use technology.

[PAUSE FOR YOU TO ANSWER]

Part 2

Track 28

Examiner:	Now, in this part of the test you are going to talk together. Here are some pictures that show different types of entertainment. Do you like these different types of entertainment? Say why or why not. I'll say that again. Do you like these different types of entertainment? Say why or why not. All right? Now, talk together.
Candidate A:	I like going to the cinema to watch the latest films. How about you?

[PAUSE FOR YOU TO ANSWER]

Candidate A	Why do you like that?

[PAUSE FOR YOU TO ANSWER]

Candidate A	I like watching films because it's a good way to forget about your everyday life and worries for a few hours. Sometimes when I'm studying I need a break, so I go to the cinema with my friends and it helps me relax for a while.
Examiner:	Candidate A, do you think going to an art exhibition is fun?
Candidate A:	Yes, I think it is. It's also interesting to see different types of art. Painting is one of my hobbies, and I sometimes go to art galleries to get ideas for my own work.
Examiner:	Candidate B, do you think going to the theatre is a pleasant way to spend an evening?

[PAUSE FOR YOU TO ANSWER]

Examiner:	So Candidate A, which of these types of entertainment do you like the least?
Candidate A:	Well, I don't really like playing video games. I think they're boring and it isn't good for you to sit in front of a screen for many hours and not get any exercise.
Examiner:	And you, Candidate B, which of these types of entertainment do you like the least?

[PAUSE FOR YOU TO ANSWER]

Examiner:	Thank you.
Examiner:	Now, do you prefer spending time with your friends and family or on your own, Candidate B?

[PAUSE FOR YOU TO ANSWER]

Examiner: Why is that, Candidate B?

[PAUSE FOR YOU TO ANSWER]

Examiner: And what about you, Candidate A? Do you prefer spending time with your friends and family or on your own?

Candidate A: Sometimes it's nice to do things with other people because it's more fun to do things together. And they can help you if you have any problems. But sometimes I also like to be by myself and read books or paint.

Examiner: Do you prefer indoor entertainment or having fun outdoors, Candidate A?

Candidate A: I prefer indoor entertainment, like going to the cinema, but I also enjoy going out and meeting new people. I meet lots of people like me when I go to art galleries.

Examiner: And you, Candidate B? Do you prefer entertainment inside or having fun outdoors?

[PAUSE FOR YOU TO ANSWER]

Examiner: Why is that, Candidate B?

[PAUSE FOR YOU TO ANSWER]

Examiner: Thank you. That is the end of the test.

TEST 5   LISTENING

Part 1

Track 29

Key English Test, Listening
There are five parts to the test. You will hear each piece twice.
We will now stop for a moment.
Please ask any questions now, because you must not speak during the test.
Now look at the instructions for Part 1.
For each question, choose the correct answer.
Look at Question 1.

1 *What will they buy Timmy for his birthday?*

Man: Timmy's birthday is next week! Shall we get him those football boots he wants?

Woman: He's also asking for jeans ... and a shirt.

Man: He can't have everything! What about asking your parents to give him the boots?

Woman: OK, so we could get the jeans and a shirt.

Man: Just the jeans. They're quite expensive. He can wait for the shirt.

Woman: OK.

Now listen again.

2 *What time will they meet?*

Ted: Would you like to meet for a coffee later?

Ella: OK. What about eleven?

Ted: Eleven? My doctor's appointment is at ten. That should take about thirty minutes.

Ella: Well, if you come out at half past ten, you've got half an hour to get to the café.

Ted: OK, that should be fine.

Ella: Great. See you then. Usual place.

Now listen again.

3 *Where will they go skiing?*

Man: ... France has lots of places for skiing

Woman: France? Again! We were there last year. What about a change. Italy? Or Poland? I hear that's cheap.

Man: But France has the best skiing. And I want to use my French.

Woman: If you let me choose the hotel, then OK. If not, then I say Italy.

Man: Agreed. You can choose where we stay.

Now listen again.

4 *How will the friends travel?*

Man: Shall we get a taxi?

Woman: The last time I tried that I waited for half an hour.

Man: Let's take the car then.

Woman: It's difficult to park in town. Let's jump on a bus.

Man: But there aren't many around at this time of day.

Woman: So what about driving after all? We just have to hope we find a space.

Man: Fine.

Now listen again.

5 *How much will the woman pay for the bicycle?*

Woman: How much do you want for the bicycle?

Man: Fifty pounds.

Woman: I'm sorry, that's too expensive. Will you take forty?

Man: I won't sell it if I can't get fifty pounds for it.

Woman: I can't afford fifty. Forty-five pounds is my last offer.

Man: That's no good.

Woman: OK, you win! But forty-five pounds would be fairer. Now give me the bike.

Now listen again.
That is the end of Part 1.

Part 2

Track 30

Now look at Part 2.
For each question, write the correct answer in the gap.
Write one word or a number or a date or a time. Look at questions 6–10 now.

You have ten seconds.

You will hear a speaker giving information about a skiing trip.

Woman:	Thanks for coming today and showing interest in the skiing trip. Now, I'm going to give you some details. This year we're going to Italy.
	The trip starts on the second of January and lasts for ten days, so we'll be away until the twelfth of January. I'm pleased to say that this year trip will be a bit less expensive than last year, when it was £775. The price has come down £45 to £730, and that's because the hotel is cheaper.
	That price includes breakfast, the evening meal, the cost of renting skis and ski clothes, and the ski lifts. But you'll need to pay for your own lunch. That's not included, and drinks aren't, either.
	There are lessons every morning. The cost is included in the price of the holiday. If you're a beginner, I strongly advise you to take these lessons so that you learn good skiing techniques. Right, are there any questions?

Now listen again.
That is the end of Part 2.

Part 3

Track 31

Now look at Part 3.

For each question, choose the correct answer. Look at questions 11–15 now. You have twenty seconds. .
You will hear Nigel talking to his friend Elizabeth about his course at university.

Elizabeth:	Hi Nigel. How's your course?
Nigel:	OK, I think. It's harder than I expected but I've got some friends who are doing the same course. I'm glad because we help each other study. But there's no spare time left for my other friends! My best friends are doing other courses.
Elizabeth:	Jenny does Business too, doesn't she?
Nigel:	Yes. We're working on a project together. But it's only us and Pete at the moment. We need another person in our group.
Elizabeth:	What do you have to do in the project?
Nigel:	We have to start a company and make money!
Elizabeth:	Doing what?
Nigel:	We still haven't decided. I'm interested in selling something, maybe through the student shop.
Elizabeth:	What sort of thing?
Nigel:	Maybe something students use, like pens, notebooks, bags. Jenny's

talking about food or drink, but I'm not interested.

Elizabeth:	Maybe you should think about it for a few days. You might have clearer ideas then. Selling things to students is hard – they don't have much money, so it must be something that they really want!

Now listen again.
That is the end of Part 3.

Part 4

Track 32

Now look at Part 4.
For each question, choose the correct answer.

16 *You will hear a woman talking to a friend about an experience. Where did she go?*

Woman:	It was fantastic! Really! And the story was so exciting. We were close to the stage so we had a great view. The costumes were amazing. I've never been to one before. It's quite hard to follow what's going on because there's only singing, so you have to pay attention.

Now listen again.

17 *You will hear a man and a woman talking. Where has the man been?*

Woman:	Oh, you're back. Did you have a good time?
Man:	Well, Barney fell into the water and got wet, so then he wanted to come home.
Woman:	Is he OK? How did that happen?
Man:	He wasn't careful! I told him he was too close to the water. And we didn't catch anything either.
Woman:	Oh, that's a pity.

Now listen again.

18 *You will hear a man and a woman talking. What will they have for breakfast?*

Woman:	Do you want some cereal for breakfast?
Man:	Cereal? We need something to keep us going all day. We can't stop for lunch. What about some eggs, toast and mushrooms?
Woman:	Eggs, then, with toast. Mushrooms take too long, and we need to leave soon.
Man:	OK, but I'm having a big cooked breakfast tomorrow with eggs, mushrooms, toast *and* cereal.

Now listen again.

19 *You will hear two friends talking. What did Karen want to buy?*

Man:	Did you get everything you wanted, Karen?
Karen:	Nearly. I couldn't find a blouse I liked. I tried on one or two.
Man:	Did you try that shop we saw yesterday? Next to the book shop?

| Karen: | Yes, I did, but they didn't have anything I liked. So I bought a book instead. Then we had a nice lunch – bread and soup. |
| Man: | Good. |

Now listen again.

20 *You will hear two friends talking. What new piece of furniture has David got?*

Woman:	Oh, that's nice, David.
David:	Do you like it?
Woman:	It goes really well in this room.
David:	Well, it'll be useful when I invite lots of people to my new flat. We can all sit down together.
Woman:	You can have dinner parties!
David:	It's big enough for six people. I just need more chairs now.

Now listen again.
That is the end of Part 4.

Part 5

Track 33

Now look at Part 5.
For each question, choose the correct answer.
Look at Questions 21 to 25 now.
You have 15 seconds.
You will hear Paul and Donna talking about summer jobs. What job does each person have?

Paul:	Have you got a job for the summer, Donna?
Donna:	Yes, I'm going to work for my parents, serving customers. I'll probably also have to help with the washing-up in the kitchen.
Paul:	That'll keep you busy!
Donna:	Yes, but it'll be fun.
Paul:	What about Clare and Kevin? Have they got jobs?
Donna:	Clare's doing her usual job in the countryside – picking fruit and looking after the animals. And Kevin's going to work at his uncle's hotel.
Paul:	Again? I wouldn't like to tidy people's rooms and empty their bins! Poor Kevin!
Donna:	What about you, Paul?
Paul:	I'm back at the language school this summer. We've got some French teenagers arriving on Saturday for an English course.
Donna:	Do you know what the others are doing? Tony and Katherine?
Paul:	Tony's going to Rome for the summer. His parents have got a small hotel there.
Donna:	So he'll be working as a receptionist?
Paul:	He usually does. But this year he's going to show tourists around the sights of Rome. You know how he loves talking! And Katherine will be at her local newspaper again, writing articles. What a great job!

Now listen again.
That is the end of Part 5. You now have six minutes to write your answers on the answer sheet.
That is the end of the test.

TEST 5   SPEAKING

Part 1

Track 34

Examiner:	Good afternoon. Can I have your mark sheets, please? I'm David Wheeler and this is Brenda Jones. What's your name please, Candidate A?
Candidate A:	My name's Adolfo da Silva.
Examiner:	And what's your name please, Candidate B?
[PAUSE FOR YOU TO ANSWER]	
Examiner:	Candidate B, do you work or are you a student?
[PAUSE FOR YOU TO ANSWER]	
Examiner:	Where do you live, Candidate B?
[PAUSE FOR YOU TO ANSWER]	
Examiner:	Thank you. Candidate A, do you work or are you a student?
Candidate A:	I work.
Examiner:	Where do you live?
Candidate A:	I live in Alfama, south of the city centre.
Examiner:	Thank you.
Examiner:	Now, let's talk about food. Candidate A, what is your favourite food?
Candidate A:	I love my mother's food. She's a very good cook.
Examiner:	What do you eat in the morning?
Candidate A:	I usually have a cup of coffee with milk. I also have some toast with ham and cheese.
Examiner:	Candidate B, what can you cook?
[PAUSE FOR YOU TO ANSWER]	
Examiner:	And Candidate B what do you like to eat when you go to a restaurant?
[PAUSE FOR YOU TO ANSWER]	
Examiner:	Now Candidate A, please tell me what you eat at home on a special day.
Candidate A:	On special days I sit down with my family and we eat together. We always have a bean dish – we call it *feijoada* – with meat and fish. There is rice and bread to go with it.
Examiner:	Now, let's talk about shopping. Candidate B, what kind of shopping do you like?
[PAUSE FOR YOU TO ANSWER]	

Examiner:	Who do you go shopping with, Candidate B?
[PAUSE FOR YOU TO ANSWER]	
Examiner:	Candidate A, do you prefer small local shops or big shops when you go shopping?
Candidate A:	I prefer going to the shopping centre with big shops.
Examiner:	How often do you go shopping?
Candidate A:	Not very often. I don't like it very much. I prefer to do other things.
Examiner:	Now Candidate B, please tell me about going shopping when you need clothes. Where do you go?
[PAUSE FOR YOU TO ANSWER]	

Part 2

Track 35

Examiner:	Now, in this part of the test you are going to talk together. Here are some pictures that show different presents for a teenager. Do you like these different presents for a teenager? Say why or why not. I'll say that again. Do you like these different presents for a teenager? Say why or why not. All right? Now, talk together.
Candidate A:	I think a bicycle is a very good present. It's healthy for young people to go out on their bike. What do you think?
[PAUSE FOR YOU TO ANSWER]	
Candidate A	I think a laptop is a really good idea for a present for a teenager. I think a teenager would be very happy to get one. Do you agree?
[PAUSE FOR YOU TO ANSWER]	
Candidate A:	A mobile phone is a good present for an older teenager, but for a younger one, it might not be a good idea.
[PAUSE FOR YOU TO ANSWER]	
Candidate A:	Now books, ... Hmm. I think a young teenager might think it's boring to get books.
[PAUSE FOR YOU TO ANSWER]	
Candidate A:	You're right. Now, a guitar. I think learning a musical instrument is a fun thing to do, so a guitar is a good idea for a present.
[PAUSE FOR YOU TO ANSWER]	
Examiner:	Candidate A, do you think a bicycle might be a dangerous present?
Candidate A	Not really. If you are careful, then a bike is OK, but I think you should

	have lessons on how to cycle safely.
Examiner:	Candidate B, do you think some people might think a laptop is not a good present?
[PAUSE FOR YOU TO ANSWER]	
Examiner:	So Candidate A, which of these presents do you think is the best for a teenager?
Candidate A:	I think a bicycle is the best present.
Examiner:	And you, Candidate B, which of these presents do you think is the best?
[PAUSE FOR YOU TO ANSWER]	
Examiner:	Thank you.
Examiner:	Now, would you prefer a laptop or a mobile phone as a present, Candidate B?
[PAUSE FOR YOU TO ANSWER]	
Examiner:	Why is that Candidate B?
[PAUSE FOR YOU TO ANSWER]	
Examiner:	And what about you, Candidate A? Would you prefer books or a guitar for a present?
Candidate A:	I'd prefer a guitar. I can get books from the library, but I've never played a musical instrument, and I'd like to try.
Examiner:	Do you like cycling, Candidate A?
Candidate A:	Yes, I do.
Examiner:	Why?
Candidate A:	It's quick and easy to get somewhere. But it's not good if it's raining.
Examiner:	Do you like reading, Candidate B?
[PAUSE FOR YOU TO ANSWER]	
Examiner:	Thank you. That is the end of the test.

TEST 6   LISTENING

Part 1

Track 36

Key English Test, Listening
There are five parts to the test. You will hear each piece twice.
We will now stop for a moment.
Please ask any questions now, because you must not speak during the test.
Now look at the instructions for Part 1.
For each question, choose the correct answer.
Look at Question 1.

1 *Where were the sunglasses the last time Mark saw them?*

Woman:	Mark, have you seen my sunglasses?
Mark:	You had them on Saturday at the beach. They were in your backpack.

Woman:	I've looked. They aren't there.
Mark:	What about on your desk? You often put things there.
Woman:	Good idea. I'll look now.
Mark:	Oh, and look on the bookcase, too. Maybe you put them there with your keys.

Now listen again.

2 *Where did the man see the ad for the concert?*

Man:	Hey, Sandy, are you going to the concert in the park this year?
Sandy:	I haven't heard anything about a concert!
Man:	That's strange. Tina usually puts ads about local events on the noticeboard.
Sandy:	I'd love to go. Where can we get tickets?
Man:	The ad in the newspaper this morning said we can get them online.
Sandy:	Great. I can't wait.

Now listen again.

3 *Who is Simon?*

Woman:	Thanks for coming to the party, David.
David:	It's nice to be here!
Woman:	Come and meet my brother Simon. He's over there.
David:	Is he the guy with the dark hair and the blue jacket?
Woman:	No, that's my cousin Max. My brother is the one with the dark hair and shirt talking to the tall man with the glasses.
David:	I'll go and say hi.

Now listen again.

4 *What job does the woman want help with?*

Man:	Tanya, do you need any help? I can wash the dirty dishes for you.
Tanya:	Don't worry. I've already put them in the dishwasher.
Man:	How about if I cut up those vegetables next to the cooker?
Tanya:	Ah, great, that would be a big help. Thank you! And the kids can put away the dishes when they come out of the dishwasher.

Now listen again.

5 *When might the next bus arrive?*

Woman:	Excuse me, what time is the next bus?
Man:	It usually comes at twenty-five past three, but the buses are running about twenty minutes late today.
Woman:	Really? So it will be here at quarter to four ... I need to be at the dentist at four.
Man:	Maybe you should take a taxi.
Woman:	I will. It takes about half an hour to get to the dentist by bus.

Now listen again.
That is the end of Part 1.

Part 2

Track 37

Now look at Part 2.
For each question, write the correct answer in the gap. Write one word or a number or a date or a time. Look at questions 6–10 now.
You have ten seconds.
You will hear a tour guide talking about a boat tour in Venice.

Woman:	Welcome aboard! Before we begin our tour, let me tell you a few things about this beautiful city. Venice is built on a number of islands in the Adriatic Sea. No one knows the exact number, but we think there are 118. Between the islands there are 150 canals.
	Today we are going to travel along the Grand Canal, the city's busiest canal. It's also the longest: almost four kilometres long! You won't see any cars, of course, but there will be lots of different boats.
	We will pass under four bridges, but there are many more in the city. Venice has 391 bridges, and most of them are very beautiful. You should try and see some of them while you are here.
	Our boat trip today will take about thirty minutes. We will go past many of the city's famous churches, museums and palaces. We will even go past the fish market!
	Now, please be seated and we will begin our tour ... [fade]

Now listen again.
That is the end of Part 2.

Part 3

Track 38

Now look at Part 3.
For each question, choose the correct answer. Look at questions 11–15 now. You have twenty seconds.
You will hear Lisa talking to her friend Robin about finding a place to live.

Robin:	Where are you going to live while you are at university, Lisa? I'm not sure.
Lisa:	It isn't easy, is it, Robin? A secretary I spoke to told me about some university flats, but I'd also like to look online and visit some other places.
Robin:	What does the university offer?
Lisa:	There are 20 flats in an apartment building in the city centre. Four students share a flat. But I'm not sure about it. It's nine kilometres from the university. And what if I don't like the other students in the flat?
Robin:	What else is there?

Lisa: Two buildings near the university: Howard House and Morgan House. Howard House is more expensive, but there's a canteen, and the price includes meals. Morgan House is cheaper, but you only pay for your room.

Robin: So there's no canteen in Morgan House?

Lisa: That's right. But on each floor, there's a kitchen and four bathrooms – oh, and there are 25 students on each floor.

Robin: So which one do you think is better: Howard House or Morgan House?

Lisa: Well, they *sound* good, but I want to see them and meet the students who live there.

Robin: Right, because what do you do if you don't like them!

Lisa: That could be a problem ...

Now listen again.
That is the end of Part 3.

Part 4

Track 39

Now look at Part 4.
For each question, choose the correct answer.

16 *You will hear two friends talking about the weather. What is the weather going to be like tomorrow?*

Man: Do you think it will be warmer tomorrow? I'm so tired of all this rain.

Woman: Yes, I know. I can't wait until summer. It doesn't look sunny on the weather app, and the wind will be quite strong. And it's going to be rainy again at the weekend.

Man: Oh well, at least it won't be wet tomorrow!

Now listen again.

17 *You will hear a man talking to a friend on the phone. Why is he angry?*

Man: You won't believe it! You know the suit I wore to the meeting last week? I took it to the dry cleaner's and they said they could clean it in an hour, so I went to a café to wait. When I returned, I paid and came home. But when I looked carefully at the suit, it was still dirty! I paid a lot of money for nothing!

Now listen again.

18 *You will hear a woman talking to her friend about work. Why is she unhappy?*

Man: Do you have any holidays planned, Michelle?

Michelle: No, unfortunately. I have to work on Saturday and Sunday twice this month, and I'm not pleased about that.

Man: So, how many hours a week are you working now?

Michelle: About 20 hours, but I also work a couple of evenings in the week.

Now listen again.

19 *You will hear a man talking to his friend about where he lives. What does he say about it?*

Woman: Where do you live now, Chris?

Chris: On the other side of town. I share a house with two other people.

Woman: Do you like it there?

Chris: Yes and no. I need thirty minutes to cycle here in the morning – the traffic is terrible.

Woman: So why did you move far from work?

Chris: The city centre was too noisy for me.

Now listen again.

20 *You will hear two friends talking about a sports centre. Which sport is the woman going to do?*

Man: So, are you going to become a member of the sports centre?

Woman: Yes. Actually, I joined last week. I was quite good at football at school, and I'd love to play with the local team here. But maybe I'll try another ball game, too.

Man: How about volleyball or tennis?

Woman: I've never tried them, but I'll think about it.

Now listen again.
That is the end of Part 4.

Part 5

Track 40

Now look at Part 5.
For each question, choose the correct answer.
Look at Questions 21 to 25 now.
You have 15 seconds.

You will hear Charlie talking to his friend Evie about visiting his family. What gift did he buy for each person?

Evie: When are you going home, Charlie?

Charlie: Tomorrow, and I've bought everyone a gift. Look!

Evie: Who are these for?

Charlie: Granny. Her hands get cold in the winter, and these will keep them nice and warm.

Evie: Is the scarf for her, too?

Charlie: No, that's for Grandad. I also got him this – he needs a new one. He lost his wallet last month.

Evie: Nice ... What did you get your mum?

Charlie: I bought her these earrings ... and this bracelet.

Evie: Oh, Charlie, they're beautiful!

Charlie: They're a special gift because it's her birthday tomorrow.

Evie: What about your dad?

Charlie: I got him this. Everyone else in my family listens to music on their phones, but not Dad. He'll also enjoy listening to the news on it in the mornings.

Evie: And your brother?

Charlie: Oh, he's football mad. I was going to get him a football shirt, but then I saw this. It's a history of his team and there are some great photos in it.

Evie: What about your sister?

Charlie: This. It's bigger than her school bag and she can put all her books and lots of things in it.

Evie: I love the colours.

Now listen again.
That is the end of Part 5. You now have six minutes to write your answers on the answer sheet.
That is the end of the test.

TEST 6   SPEAKING

Part 1

Track 41

Examiner: Good evening.
Can I have your mark sheets, please?
I'm Valerie Walker. And this is James Liddell.
What's your name, Candidate A?

Candidate A: My name's Vittoria Conti.

Examiner: And what's your name, Candidate B?

[PAUSE FOR YOU TO ANSWER]

Examiner: Candidate B, do you work or are you a student?

[PAUSE FOR YOU TO ANSWER]

Examiner: Where do you come from, Candidate B?

[PAUSE FOR YOU TO ANSWER]

Examiner: Thank you.
Candidate A, do you work or are you a student?

Candidate A: I'm a student.

Examiner: Where do you come from?

Candidate A: I come from Lugano in Switzerland.

Examiner: Thank you.

Examiner: Now, let's talk about hobbies. Candidate A, what hobbies do you do during the week?

Candidate A: One of my hobbies is music. I play the guitar in a band, and I usually practise every evening after college.

Examiner: What activities did you do last weekend?

Candidate A: I went camping with some friends at the weekend. We stayed in tents at a campsite in the forest. We often go camping there because we hike in the mountains.

Examiner: Candidate B, what hobbies do you have?

[PAUSE FOR YOU TO ANSWER]

Examiner: How often are you able to do this, Candidate B?

[PAUSE FOR YOU TO ANSWER]

Examiner: Now Candidate A, please tell me something about what activities you like to do with your family.

Candidate A: At the weekend I like to go cycling with my brother. My family and I also enjoy having barbecues on a Saturday afternoon if the weather is nice.

Examiner: Now, let's talk about clothes. Candidate B, what clothes do you wear every day?

[PAUSE FOR YOU TO ANSWER]

Examiner: And Candidate B what colours do you like for clothes?

[PAUSE FOR YOU TO ANSWER]

Examiner: Candidate A, what clothes do you wear when you go to a party?

Candidate A: I usually wear a dress, a jacket and smart shoes. I also sometimes wear trousers with a blouse.

Examiner: How often do you buy clothes?

Candidate A: I usually buy clothes once a month when I go shopping with my friends. If I need something, I'll buy it sooner. I try not to buy clothes very often.

Examiner: Now Candidate B, please tell me something about the clothes you like to buy.

[PAUSE FOR YOU TO ANSWER]

Part 2

Track 42

Examiner: Now, in this part of the test you are going to talk together.
Here are some pictures that show different outdoor activities.
Do you like these different outdoor activities? Say why or why not. I'll say that again.
Do you like these different outdoor activities? Say why or why not.
All right? Now, talk together.

Candidate A: I like a few of these. I like to be active and go outside with my friends so I've done many of these activities. How about you?

[PAUSE FOR YOU TO ANSWER]

Candidate A Do you ever have picnics in the park?

[PAUSE FOR YOU TO ANSWER]

Candidate A I really enjoy having picnics and eating outside with my family or friends. We usually take food with us in a basket when we go walking in the countryside. When we find a nice place, we sit and eat our food.

Examiner: Candidate A, do you think skateboarding is difficult?

Candidate A: Yes, I think it is. I tried skateboarding when I was younger, but I kept falling off. I think that if you don't wear safety clothes, you could hurt yourself.

Examiner: Candidate B, do you think swimming in a lake is dangerous?

[PAUSE FOR YOU TO ANSWER]

Examiner: So Candidate A, what do you think of music festivals?

Candidate A: I don't like them. They're noisy and there are too many people. I prefer going to concerts indoors.

Examiner: And you, Candidate B, do you think going to music festivals is fun?

[PAUSE FOR YOU TO ANSWER]

Examiner: Candidate A, which of these activities do you like best?

Candidate A: I think swimming in the lake is the best outdoor activity because it's good exercise. I enjoy swimming and I love to be close to nature.

Examiner: And you, Candidate B, which of these activities do you like best?

[PAUSE FOR YOU TO ANSWER]

Examiner: Thank you.

Examiner: Now, do you prefer being by the sea or in the mountains, Candidate B?

[PAUSE FOR YOU TO ANSWER]

Examiner: Why is that, Candidate B?

[PAUSE FOR YOU TO ANSWER]

Examiner: And what about you, Candidate A? Do you prefer being by the sea or in the mountains?

Candidate A: I prefer being in the mountains because there is lots of fresh air. I enjoy hiking and exploring the forests and looking at wildlife.

Examiner: Is it better to do sports alone or with other people, Candidate A?

Candidate A: I think it's better to do sports with other people. I like playing team sports because it's more fun to work together to win. I think it's important to spend time with other people.

Examiner: And you, Candidate B? Is it better to do sports alone or with other people?

[PAUSE FOR YOU TO ANSWER]

Examiner: Why is that, Candidate B?

[PAUSE FOR YOU TO ANSWER]

Examiner: Thank you. That is the end of the test.

TEST 7   LISTENING

Part 1

Track 43

Key English Test, Listening
There are five parts to the test. You will hear each piece twice.
We will now stop for a moment.
Please ask any questions now, because you must not speak during the test.
Now look at the instructions for Part 1.
For each question, choose the correct answer.
Look at Question 1.

1   *What time will the man pick up the woman?*

Man: What time shall I pick you up?

Woman: I've got a late meeting. I won't be finished until six o'clock.

Man: Six? I'll have to wait for half an hour. Can't you leave earlier? At five thirty?

Woman: I could probably leave at quarter to six. Can you wait for 15 minutes?

Man: OK, I might not be there by five thirty, anyway.

Now listen again.

2   *Where will they meet?*

Man: Where do you want to meet, Anne?

Woman: How about outside the cinema?

Man: But the weather's terrible. Let's meet inside somewhere. I might be late.

Woman: OK, what about the shopping centre next door? You can park the car in the car park there.

Man: Good idea.

Woman: OK, then. Just inside the main entrance.

Now listen again.

3   *What sort of holiday will they go on?*

Man: We could go to the beach for a few days.

Woman: Or something a bit different. Helen was telling me about her cycling holiday.

Man: Cycling? I cycle quite a lot at home.

Woman: Or sailing. I saw an advertisement for a sailing holiday in Turkey.

Man: You know I don't like boats. I prefer bikes to boats.

Woman: OK, let's do that, then.

Now listen again.

4   *What musical instrument will she learn to play?*

Woman: I think I'm going to learn the piano.

Man: You can practise on mine. But it's a bit old.

Woman: Thanks!

Man: I've got a guitar too, if you want to use it.

Woman: A guitar? I tried that, but I wasn't very good. I also tried the violin.

Man: I love the violin. Why don't you try again?

Woman: I want something easier.

Now listen again.

5 *What date is the man's appointment with the dentist?*

Woman: Can you come on the fourteenth?

Man: Yes, but only after two o'clock.

Woman: Oh dear. How about the next day?

Man: The fifteenth? I'm free in the morning. But the day after that, I'm free all day.

Woman: All day?

Man: Yes.

Woman: How about eleven o'clock in the morning?

Man: Perfect.

Now listen again.

That is the end of Part 1.

Part 2

Track 44

Now look at Part 2.

For each question, write the correct answer in the gap. Write one word or a number or a date or a time. Look at questions 6–10 now.

You have ten seconds.

You will hear a speaker giving information to university students about evening language classes.

Woman: Welcome to the University Language Centre. I'd like to give you some basic information about our evening language classes.

We offer evening classes in English, Italian, French, Russian and Spanish. Classes are in the afternoons or evenings, and they start in the first week of October. Courses are six weeks long, so they end in the middle of November. The English courses are free, but the other language courses cost £80. If you want to learn more than one language, you get a 20% discount, so your second course will cost you just £64.

There are courses for beginners as well as for more advanced students. Most courses have lessons three times a week, but English courses have four lessons a week, so 24 lessons in total. You don't need to buy any books, but we suggest that all students should bring a notebook and a pen or pencil to classes. Now, any questions?

Now listen again.

That is the end of Part 2.

Part 3

Track 45

Now look at Part 3.

For each question, choose the correct answer. Look at questions 11–15 now. You have twenty seconds.

You will hear Paul talking to his friend Debbie about his new job.

Debbie: Hi Paul. How's your new job?

Paul: Hi Debbie. Really good. My new colleagues are fun to work with.

Debbie: Do you miss your old colleagues?

Paul: Well, that was the problem with my old job. I almost never saw anyone else.

Debbie: I expect it's a big change. What are you doing now?

Paul: I'm in the office. When customers come in, I give them some documents to complete, check their driving licence, answer any questions, take their money, and give them the keys for the car they're renting.

Debbie: Is it a difficult job?

Paul: No, the job is simple. But when there are a lot of customers and people have to wait for their car, they can get angry.

Debbie: How many people work there?

Paul: There are six of us in the office. Then there are nine people who work outside, getting the cars ready, making sure they've got petrol, showing customers how things work, …

Debbie: It sounds better than your last job.

Paul: It is. I don't make as much money now, but that's because I'm new. But soon I'll be earning more than I was.

Now listen again.

That is the end of Part 3.

Part 4

Track 46

Now look at Part 4.

For each question, choose the correct answer.

16 *You will hear a woman talking about her day. Where did she go?*

Woman: I had a lovely afternoon on my own. You know what it's like – on a weekday there's almost no one else there. I spent a long time just sitting and looking at one old painting. It was so quiet! I wrote my name in the visitors' book and said how much I enjoyed it.

Now listen again.

17 *You will hear a man talking. What has he lost?*

Man: I can't believe it! I parked my car late last night in the rain and I didn't notice the name of the street. I couldn't find it today until I had looked for it for 30 minutes! Then my money and my keys were missing. My money was in my coat pocket, but I don't know about my keys.

Now listen again.

18 *You will hear two friends talking. What will they do this afternoon?*

Woman: Would you like to watch the football game?

Man:	We could, but everyone knows who will win. What about a game of tennis?
Woman:	But it looks like rain! I'd like to watch the game.
Man:	Or we could watch that film we were talking about?
Woman:	If you agree to the football, we can watch the film another time.
Man:	OK, then.

Now listen again.

19 *You will hear two friends talking. What will they have for dinner?*

Man:	Shall we get a pizza?
Woman:	Didn't we have one a few nights ago?
Man:	Or fish and chips?
Woman:	The fish and chip shop is closed on Tuesdays. We haven't had a curry for a long time.
Man:	I don't like hot food. We have pizza often because we like it.
Woman:	All right, but it's curry or fish and chips the next time!

Now listen again.

20 *You will hear a man talking in a shop. What is he looking at?*

Woman:	Can I help you sir?
Man:	Yes, I'm interested in this. The sound is good, but do you have one with a bigger screen?
Woman:	The bigger ones are over here.
Man:	I like that one. That would be good for watching things on.
Woman:	Yes, it's a popular model. And it has more memory than the one here.

Now listen again.
That is the end of Part 4.

Part 5

Track 47

Now look at Part 5.
For each question, choose the correct answer.
Look at Questions 21 to 25 now.
You have 15 seconds.

You will hear Dean and Kylie planning the final week of their holiday. What activity will they do on each day?

Dean:	It's Sunday already! Let's plan our last week.
Kylie:	Well, we can go to the museum tomorrow.
Dean:	Yes, and on Tuesday we could do something for the children. They'd love to see all the baby animals, especially the elephants.
Kylie:	Good idea. And they want to visit Aqualand too.
Dean:	Let's keep that for Saturday.

Kylie:	So what about looking around the old town on Wednesday? We can join a group and there will be someone to show us around and tell us about the history of the place.
Dean:	Yeah, OK. And I really want to go shopping.
Kylie:	OK, but let's look around before we buy anything.
Dean:	Good idea. Well, on Thursday, we could go on a boat trip, or visit the palace or go to the fish market.
Kylie:	We can't do all those things, but I'd love to look at all the seafood for sale.
Dean:	Yes, that would be fun.
Kylie:	And then on Friday we can buy gifts for the neighbours ... and I saw some lovely jewellery...
Dean:	And the kids can go swimming on Saturday.
Kylie:	Done!

Now listen again.
That is the end of Part 5. You now have six minutes to write your answers on the answer sheet.
That is the end of the test.

TEST 7   SPEAKING

Part 1

Track 48

Examiner:	Good morning.
	Can I have your mark sheets, please?
	I'm Jack Rider. And this is Linda Smith.
	Candidate A, what's your name, please?
Candidate A:	My name's Chiara Bianchi.
Examiner:	And Candidate B, what's your name, please?
[PAUSE FOR YOU TO ANSWER]	
Examiner:	Candidate B, do you work or are you a student?
[PAUSE FOR YOU TO ANSWER]	
Examiner:	Where do you live, Candidate B?
[PAUSE FOR YOU TO ANSWER]	
Examiner:	Thank you.
	Candidate A, do you work or are you a student?
Candidate A:	I'm a student.
Examiner:	Where do you live?
Candidate A:	I also live in Naples. In Soccavo, in the west of the city.
Examiner:	Thank you.
Examiner:	Now, let's talk about the weather.
	Candidate A, what is the weather like in the summer where you live?
Candidate A:	It's really hot in Naples in the summer. It's often over 31 or 32 degrees, so you can't stay in the sun for a long time.

Examiner:	What about the winter?
Candidate A:	It doesn't often get very cold, and it almost never snows.
Examiner:	Candidate B, what sort of weather do you like?

[PAUSE FOR YOU TO ANSWER]

Examiner:	What do you do when the weather is good, Candidate B?

[PAUSE FOR YOU TO ANSWER]

Examiner:	Now Candidate A, please tell me what sort of weather you don't like.
Candidate A:	I don't like it when it rains. I hate getting wet. It's worse when it's windy as well. Then you can't use an umbrella and everything gets wet. When my hair gets wet, it looks terrible!
Examiner:	Now, let's talk about school. Candidate B, what was your school like?

[PAUSE FOR YOU TO ANSWER]

Examiner:	What was your favourite subject, Candidate B?

[PAUSE FOR YOU TO ANSWER]

Examiner:	Candidate A, what did you like about your school?
Candidate A:	We had a friendly head teacher. She helped everyone to do their best.
Examiner:	Was there anything you didn't like about your school?
Candidate A:	We always had a lot of homework and I didn't like doing it, especially at the weekend and in the evenings.
Examiner:	Now Candidate B, please tell me about a good teacher that you can remember from school.

[PAUSE FOR YOU TO ANSWER]

Part 2

Track 49

Examiner:	Now, in this part of the test you are going to talk together. Here are some pictures that show different jobs. Do you like these different jobs? Say why or why not. I'll say that again. Do you like these different jobs? Say why or why not. All right? Now, talk together.
Candidate A:	I think a teacher is a good job because you can help young children learn. This is very important. What do you think about being a teacher?

[PAUSE FOR YOU TO ANSWER]

Candidate A	What do you think about being a cook?

[PAUSE FOR YOU TO ANSWER]

Candidate A:	I agree. But I think a dentist is a good job and it's also useful. Everybody needs dentists.

[PAUSE FOR YOU TO ANSWER]

Candidate A:	I'm not sure about a firefighter. What do you think about that?

[PAUSE FOR YOU TO ANSWER]

Candidate A:	The last job is a mechanic. I don't think I'd like to be one. It's a hard job and you get very dirty when you work with cars all day.

[PAUSE FOR YOU TO ANSWER]

Examiner:	Candidate A, do you think being a dentist is interesting?
Candidate A:	Yes, I do.
Examiner:	Why?
Candidate A:	You meet different people. Also, everybody's teeth are different, so you see something different every day. It's never boring.
Examiner:	Candidate B, do you think being a cook is interesting?

[PAUSE FOR YOU TO ANSWER]

Examiner:	So Candidate A, which of these jobs do you like the best?
Candidate A:	I think being a dentist is the best job.
Examiner:	And you, Candidate B, which of these jobs do you like the best?

[PAUSE FOR YOU TO ANSWER]

Examiner:	Thank you.
Examiner:	Now, Candidate B, which job do you think is better, a mechanic or a firefighter?

[PAUSE FOR YOU TO ANSWER]

Examiner:	Why is that, Candidate B?

[PAUSE FOR YOU TO ANSWER]

Examiner:	And what about you, Candidate A? Which job do you think is better, a cook or a firefighter?
Candidate A:	I think a cook is a better job than a firefighter. A cook can sometimes prepare new dishes. When you are a firefighter, you have to be ready to go to work at any time because a fire can start in the middle of the night.
Examiner:	Which job do you think is the worst job, Candidate A?
Candidate A:	Being a mechanic.
Examiner:	Why?
Candidate A:	I don't think it's interesting and you get very dirty.

Examiner: What do you think is the worst job, Candidate B?

[PAUSE FOR YOU TO ANSWER]

Examiner: Thank you. That is the end of the test.

TEST 8   LISTENING

Part 1

Track 50

Key English Test, Listening
There are five parts to the test. You will hear each piece twice.
We will now stop for a moment.
Please ask any questions now, because you must not speak during the test.
Now look at the instructions for Part 1.
For each question, choose the correct answer.
Look at Question 1.

1   *How long will they park for?*

Woman: Parking costs one pound for thirty minutes. Shall we pay for two hours?
Man: Let's say an hour.
Woman: We're getting you a suit. That takes a long time. We need two hours at least.
Man: I'll be finished in half an hour. Then another half an hour for the other things. We'll be back in an hour.
Woman: OK.
Now listen again.

2   *What else will they have in their picnic*

Woman: Right ... So, chicken and potato salad. What else shall we take on our picnic? Fruit? Sandwiches?
Man: We always have fruit. What about something nice, like cake?
Woman: Cake! We had cake yesterday. I can't eat *more* cake.
Man: OK, OK, you're right. Sandwiches will fill me up. If I just have fruit, I'll be hungry later.
Woman: All right.
Now listen again.

3   *What will they take to hospital for Jemima?*

Woman: We must take something when we visit Jemima in hospital.
Man: People usually take flowers.
Woman: They're boring. Why not get her a book? Then she could do some reading.
Man: But she'll have her own book. What about some chocolates?
Woman: I don't think she can eat much. Let's go with your first idea. They'll look pretty in her room.
Now listen again.

4   *Where does Alex live?*

Woman: How do we get to your house, Alex?
Alex: Go up the High Street, past the post office. Take the first turning on your left. My house is on the right-hand side of the road. You can't miss it.
Woman: I get my left and right mixed up! Turn right after the post office?
Alex: Left after the post office. Then cross the road to get to my house.
Now listen again.

5   *How much will Nicola pay for her hotel room?*

Nicola: Can I book a room for two for Friday and Saturday night, please?
Man: We have one with a king-size bed for £350.
Nicola: That's rather expensive.
Man: Or with a queen-size bed for £315. Or a room with two single beds for £279.
Nicola: Two single beds for £279?
Man: Yes.
Nicola: I'll take the one with the queen-size bed, please.
Now listen again.
That is the end of Part 1.

Part 2

Track 51

Now look at Part 2.
For each question, write the correct answer in the gap.
Write one word or a number or a date or a time. Look at questions 6–10 now.
You have ten seconds.
You will hear a speaker giving information at the start of a coach trip to London.

Woman: Good morning, everyone. My name's Michaela and I'm going to give you some information about our trip today.
It takes two hours to get to London, so that means that you will have from ten fifteen until quarter to five to look around the city. We have to leave at that time as the traffic gets very bad after five o'clock.
I know some of you want to go shopping, and the new Kings and Queens shopping centre on Bristol Street is now open. You can get a 15% discount in the shops there. I know it's not as good as the 20% we got last year, but I think you'll agree it's better than nothing. The staff there just need to see your coach ticket and they'll give you your discount.
Please be careful with your wallets and purses! The streets and shops are crowded on Saturdays, and that's a chance for pickpockets to steal things.

If you have any problems, my mobile number is 0777-5819-236. That's 0777-5819-236.

Now listen again.

That is the end of Part 2.

Part 3

Track 52

Now look at Part 3.

For each question, choose the correct answer. Look at questions 11–15 now. You have twenty seconds.
You will hear Vivien and Tom talking about their meals last night.

Vivien:	Hi Tom.
Tom:	Hi Vivien. How was your meal last night?
Vivien:	Actually, it didn't go too well. Firstly, we couldn't get around the table. We'd booked for six people, but eight came.
Tom:	Oh dear!
Vivien:	Then they didn't have anything for Monica to eat.
Tom:	She doesn't eat meat or fish, does she?
Vivien:	That's right. She's a vegetarian. She wasn't happy! Then they brought Mark the wrong dish. He ordered steak but they brought him chicken, so he sent it back, and then he had to wait again for his steak. What about your meal?
Tom:	The food was delicious, especially the dessert. Everything was perfect – until the bill arrived.
Vivien:	Was it expensive?
Tom:	Well, it was quite expensive, but we knew that from before. The problem was they gave us the bill for a different table. It took half an hour for them to fix the problem! In the end, they gave us a discount because of all the problems with the bill.
Vivien:	Well, that's something at least.

Now listen again.
That is the end of Part 3.

Part 4

Track 53

Now look at Part 4.
For each question, choose the correct answer.

16 *You will hear two friends talking. Why can't the man play football this afternoon?*

Woman:	So, are you playing football this afternoon?
Man:	I can't.
Woman:	Don't tell me. It's your foot again, isn't it?
Man:	It's true I had problems with my foot, but it's fine now. And my boss said I could leave work early to play. The trouble is I've got really bad toothache, so I'm going to see the dentist about that.

Now listen again.

17 *You will hear a man talking. What animal did he see at the zoo?*

Man:	It was just so beautiful. I watched it while it was eating. Those big teeth! I wouldn't like to be near it if it was hungry! That golden fur with the black stripes is fantastic. It must be really difficult to see it in the forest. And those yellow eyes! Just … beautiful!

Now listen again.

18 *You will hear two friends talking. Where have they been?*

Woman:	I can't believe it! They didn't have anything we wanted!
Man:	I know! I was sure they'd have some of the things on our list.
Woman:	Maybe we can find them online.
Man:	Maybe, but I hate reading on a screen all the time.
Woman:	Me too. Let's try the big one in the city centre tomorrow.

Now listen again.

19 *You will hear a woman talking. Where does her friend live?*

Woman:	I had a lovely time with Aneka. She's got a lovely place. You wouldn't know that you were in the middle of a city, it's so quiet. Her street has a village feel to it – everyone knows everyone. Then we went off to the seaside on Saturday. It took a while to get there, but it was great fun.

Now listen again.

20 *You will hear two friends talking about cooking dinner. What will the man do?*

Woman:	You have to help me!
Man:	I always do!
Woman:	Not just the easy things. The hard work is washing and cutting the vegetables. Cooking them is easy.
Man:	But I'm good at cooking.
Woman:	Well, I'm not cutting them this time.
Man:	OK, I'll do that. You do the rest.
Woman:	Fine.

Now listen again.
That is the end of Part 4.

Part 5

Track 54

Now look at Part 5.
For each question, choose the correct answer.
Look at Questions 21 to 25 now.
You have 15 seconds.
You will hear two people talking about their families. What activities do their children like?

Woman:	So, what kind of things do your children like doing?
Man:	George loves books. He reads anything.

Woman:	I wish Henry did! Henry spends all his time in front of a computer screen. I keep telling him to go outside, but he doesn't listen.
Man:	Edward was like that, but he's changed. He's on the school chess team now!
Woman:	That's great!
Man:	Yes, he loves games like chess, but he doesn't do much exercise.
Woman:	And Annabel?
Man:	She's the musician of the family. She plays in a band with some friends. They make a terrible noise! Luckily, they don't practise at our house.
Woman:	She sounds very different to my Sophie.
Man:	Is she the dancer?
Woman:	You're getting Ellie and Sophie mixed up. Sophie is the one who loves painting. She loves going to see shows with the very modern stuff, and she draws quite well herself. Ellie is the one who's always practising in her bedroom. I can hear her jumping around, and she sometimes bumps into the furniture!
Man:	We can't get any of them to do things with us.
Woman:	Same here! Not even Henry.

Now listen again.

That is the end of Part 5. You now have six minutes to write your answers on the answer sheet.

That is the end of the test.

TEST 8   SPEAKING

Part 1

Track 55

Examiner:	Good afternoon.
	Can I have your mark sheets, please?
	I'm Anita Hill. And this is Mark Flock.
	Candidate A, what's your name, please?
Candidate A:	My name's Emir Yilmaz.
Examiner:	And Candidate B, what's your name, please?
[PAUSE FOR YOU TO ANSWER]	
Examiner:	Candidate B, do you work or are you a student?
[PAUSE FOR YOU TO ANSWER]	
Examiner:	And where do you live, Candidate B?
[PAUSE FOR YOU TO ANSWER]	
Examiner:	Thank you.
	Candidate A, do you work or are you a student?
Candidate A:	I'm a student.
Examiner:	Where do you live?
Candidate A:	I live in Goztepe, too. It is an area next to Kadikoy.

Examiner:	Thank you.
Examiner:	Now, let's talk about music. Candidate A, are you a musical person?
Candidate A:	I'm not sure! I think I'm musical, but my family say I've got a terrible voice! However, I love listening to pop music on the radio.
Examiner:	Do you like music from your country?
Candidate A:	To be honest, traditional Turkish music is not my favourite. I like it, but I like Western pop music more.
Examiner:	Candidate B, what sort of music do you like?
[PAUSE FOR YOU TO ANSWER]	
Examiner:	When do you listen to music, Candidate B?
[PAUSE FOR YOU TO ANSWER]	
Examiner:	Now Candidate A, please tell me about a musical instrument you play or you would like to play.
Candidate A:	I'd like to play the guitar. My friend has one and he plays it well. It sounds really good and I wish I could play it too.
Examiner:	Now, let's talk about studying. Candidate B, where do you usually study?
[PAUSE FOR YOU TO ANSWER]	
Examiner:	Do you always study on your own, Candidate B?
[PAUSE FOR YOU TO ANSWER]	
Examiner:	Candidate A, do you study a lot online?
Candidate A:	Yes, I do. I find articles to read online and I like writing online because I can save my work easily.
Examiner:	Are there any disadvantages to studying online?
Candidate A:	Yes, if you aren't careful, you start to do other things instead of studying. For example, talking to your friends on social media.
Examiner:	Now Candidate B, please tell me how you feel about going to class with other students and listening to a teacher. Do you think that is a good way to study and to learn things?
[PAUSE FOR YOU TO ANSWER]	

Part 2

Track 56

Examiner:	Now, in this part of the test you are going to talk together.
	Here are some pictures that show different ways of getting the news.

	Do you like these different ways of getting the news? Say why or why not. I'll say that again.
	Do you like these different ways of getting the news? Say why or why not.
	All right? Now, talk together.
Candidate A:	I think a newspaper is an old-fashioned way of reading the news. What do you think?

[PAUSE FOR YOU TO ANSWER]

Candidate A	What do you think about watching the news on television?

[PAUSE FOR YOU TO ANSWER]

Candidate A:	I agree. You can also read about the news on your phone. A lot of people get news on their phone through apps, but I don't think it's easy to read stories on a small screen.

[PAUSE FOR YOU TO ANSWER]

Candidate A:	What do you think about reading the news on a laptop?

[PAUSE FOR YOU TO ANSWER]

Candidate A:	Finally, the radio. I never listen to the news on the radio. What about you?

[PAUSE FOR YOU TO ANSWER]

Examiner:	Candidate A, do you think newspapers are interesting?
Candidate A:	No, I don't.
Examiner:	Why not?
Candidate A:	It isn't up to date because the news in it is from the day before. It takes a long time to get the newspaper to the shop and for someone to buy it. So when you read it, it's already old.
Examiner:	Candidate B, do you think the news on the radio is interesting?

[PAUSE FOR YOU TO ANSWER]

Examiner:	So Candidate A, which of these ways of getting the news do you like the best?
Candidate A:	I think using a mobile phone is the best way. The screen is small, but you always have your phone with you, so you can look at it when you want.
Examiner:	And you, Candidate B, which of these ways do you like the best?

[PAUSE FOR YOU TO ANSWER]

Examiner:	Thank you.
Examiner:	Now, Candidate B, can you compare getting the news on the television with getting the news on the radio?

[PAUSE FOR YOU TO ANSWER]

Examiner:	And what about you, Candidate A? Can you compare getting the news on a phone with getting the news on a laptop?
Candidate A:	I think these are similar ways of getting the news. The difference is that you can carry your phone and look at it when you want, so you can get the news all the time, for example, when you're sitting on the bus.
Examiner:	Which of these ways of getting the news is least useful to you?
Candidate A:	Reading a newspaper.
Examiner:	Why?
Candidate A:	As I said before, the news is old. You have to read it, so it's harder than listening or watching.
Examiner:	What do you think is the least useful way to get the news, Candidate B?

[PAUSE FOR YOU TO ANSWER]

Examiner:	Thank you. That is the end of the test.

Sample answer sheets

Cambridge Assessment
English

Candidate Name		Candidate Number	
Centre Name		Centre Number	
Examination Title		Examination Details	
Candidate Signature		Assessment Date	

Supervisor: If the candidate is ABSENT or has WITHDRAWN shade here ○

Key Reading and Writing Candidate Answer Sheet

Instructions
Use a PENCIL (B or HB).
Rub out any answer you want to change with an eraser.

For Parts 1, 2, 3 and 4:
Mark ONE letter for each answer.
For example: If you think A is the right answer to
the question, mark your answer sheet like this: 0 [A● B○ C○]

For Part 5:
Write your answers clearly in the spaces next
to the numbers (25 to 30) like this:

0 | E N G L I S H

Write your answers in CAPITAL LETTERS.

Part 1		Part 2		Part 3		Part 4	
1	A B C ○○○	7	A B C ○○○	14	A B C ○○○	19	A B C ○○○
2	A B C ○○○	8	A B C ○○○	15	A B C ○○○	20	A B C ○○○
3	A B C ○○○	9	A B C ○○○	16	A B C ○○○	21	A B C ○○○
4	A B C ○○○	10	A B C ○○○	17	A B C ○○○	22	A B C ○○○
5	A B C ○○○	11	A B C ○○○	18	A B C ○○○	23	A B C ○○○
6	A B C ○○○	12	A B C ○○○			24	A B C ○○○
		13	A B C ○○○				

Part 5		Do not write below here			Do not write below here
25		25 1 0 ○ ○	28		28 1 0 ○ ○
26		26 1 0 ○ ○	29		29 1 0 ○ ○
27		27 1 0 ○ ○	30		30 1 0 ○ ○

Put your answers to Writing Parts 6 and 7 on the separate Answer Sheet

51298

Cambridge Assessment
English

Candidate Name		Candidate Number	
Centre Name		Centre Number	
Examination Title		Examination Details	
Candidate Signature		Assessment Date	

Supervisor: If the candidate is ABSENT or has WITHDRAWN shade here ○

Key Writing

Candidate Answer Sheet for Parts 6 and 7

INSTRUCTIONS TO CANDIDATES

Make sure that your name and candidate number are on this sheet.

Write your answers to Writing Parts 6 and 7 on the other side of this sheet.

Use a pencil.

You **must** write within the grey lines.

Do **not** write on the bar codes.

51298

51298

Part 6: Write your answer below.

Part 7: Write your answer below.

Examiner's Use Only

Part 6	C	O	L

Part 7	C	O	L

51298

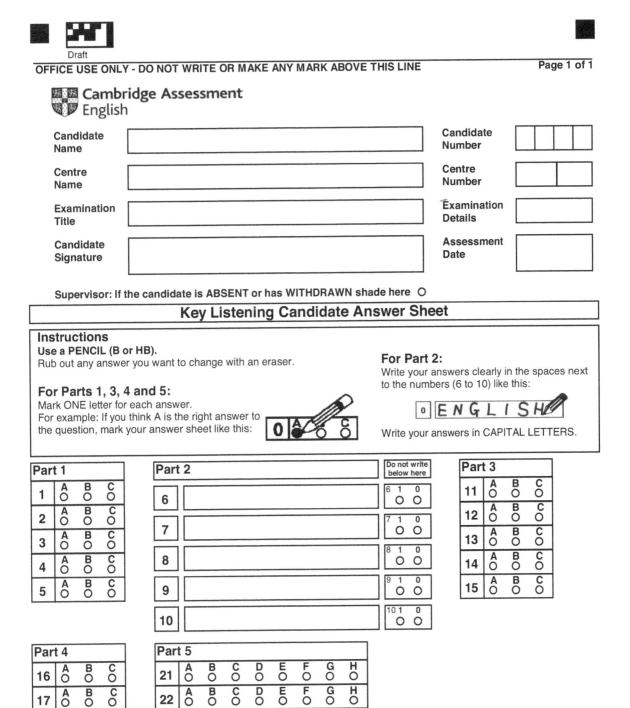

Answer key for the Reading and Listening

This is the Answer key for the Reading and Listening parts of Tests 1-8.

TEST 1

Reading

Part 1
1 C
2 B
3 A
4 A
5 B
6 C

Part 2
7 C
8 B
9 A
10 C
11 A
12 B
13 A

Part 3
14 A
15 C
16 B
17 C
18 A

Part 4
19 A
20 B
21 C
22 A
23 A
24 C

Part 5
25 you
26 on
27 at
28 to
29 let
30 something

Listening

Part 1
1 C
2 C
3 B
4 A
5 B

Part 2
6 8.30
7 6/six
8 1
9 free
10 photo

Part 3
11 A
12 C
13 B
14 B
15 C

Part 4
16 B
17 C
18 A
19 B
20 C

Part 5
21 H
22 D
23 A
24 E
25 F

TEST 2

Reading

Part 1
1 C
2 A
3 B
4 C
5 A
6 B

Part 2
7 C
8 B
9 A
10 B
11 B
12 C
13 A

Part 3
14 C
15 C
16 A
17 B
18 B

Part 4
19 C
20 A
21 B
22 B
23 A
24 C

Part 5
25 this/yesterday
26 and
27 was
28 told
29 a
30 to

Listening

Part 1
1 A
2 A
3 B
4 B
5 C

Part 2
6 China
7 4/four
8 6/six
9 games
10 July

Part 3
11 B
12 B
13 C
14 A
15 C

Part 4
16 C
17 C
18 B
19 A
20 C

Part 5
21 B
22 D
23 H
24 E
25 A

TEST 3

Reading

Part 1
1 C
2 B
3 C
4 C
5 A
6 B

Part 2
7 B
8 A
9 B
10 C
11 B
12 A
13 C

Part 3
14 A
15 C
16 B
17 B
18 A

Part 4
19 A
20 C
21 B
22 C
23 A
24 C

Part 5
25 to
26 for
27 from
28 Would
29 a
30 in

Listening

Part 1
1 B
2 A
3 C
4 B
5 A

Part 2
6 13
7 1,045
8 4/four
9 15/fifteen
10 quiet

Part 3
11 B
12 B
13 A
14 A
15 B

Part 4
16 C
17 C
18 B
19 B
20 A

Part 5
21 D
22 A
23 H
24 C
25 G

TEST 4

Reading

Part 1
1 B
2 A
3 B
4 C
5 C
6 B

Part 2
7 B
8 C
9 A
10 C
11 A
12 B
13 C

Part 3
14 C
15 C
16 C
17 A
18 B

Part 4
19 B
20 C
21 A
22 C
23 B
24 A

Part 5
25 to
26 a
27 them
28 are
29 and
30 next/close

Listening

Part 1
1 A
2 B
3 C
4 B
5 B

Part 2
6 February
7 40,000
8 Park
9 died
10 1931

Part 3
11 B
12 C
13 A
14 B
15 A

Part 4
16 A
17 B
18 B
19 B
20 C

Part 5
21 H
22 C
23 D
24 A
25 E

TEST 5

Reading

Part 1
1 C
2 B
3 B
4 A
5 C
6 C

Part 2
7 B
8 C
9 B
10 B
11 A
12 C
13 A

Part 3
14 C
15 C
16 A
17 C
18 B

Part 4
19 C
20 A
21 C
22 A
23 A
24 B

Part 5
25 to
26 a
27 on
28 the
29 like
30 next

Listening

Part 1
1 B
2 A
3 A
4 B
5 C

Part 2
6 12th
7 730
8 drinks
9 morning
10 beginners

Part 3
11 A
12 C
13 C
14 C
15 B

Part 4
16 C
17 A
18 B
19 A
20 B

Part 5
21 F
22 A
23 H
24 E
25 C

TEST 6

Reading

Part 1
1 A
2 C
3 C
4 B
5 B
6 A

Part 2
7 A
8 C
9 A
10 A
11 B
12 A
13 B

Part 3
14 A
15 C
16 A
17 A
18 B

Part 4
19 C
20 A
21 B
22 B
23 C
24 A

Part 5
25 ever
26 because/as
27 and
28 been/ridden
29 the
30 some/my

Listening

Part 1
1 B
2 C
3 B
4 A
5 C

Part 2
6 118
7 4/four
8 391
9 30/thirty
10 fish

Part 3
11 B
12 C
13 A
14 B
15 A

Part 4
16 B
17 A
18 A
19 C
20 C

Part 5
21 E
22 G
23 A
24 B
25 D

TEST 7

Reading

Part 1
1 B
2 A
3 B
4 C
5 A
6 C

Part 2
7 B
8 B
9 C
10 B
11 A
12 B
13 A

Part 3
14 C
15 A
16 B
17 A
18 C

Part 4
19 C
20 A
21 B
22 C
23 A
24 B

Part 5
25 the
26 would
27 will
28 going
29 of
30 let

Listening

Part 1
1 B
2 C
3 B
4 A
5 C

Part 2
6 first
7 80
8 64
9 24
10 notebook

Part 3
11 C
12 B
13 C
14 A
15 B

Part 4
16 A
17 B
18 A
19 C
20 B

Part 5
21 H
22 D
23 F
24 A
25 C

TEST 8

Reading

Part 1
1 C
2 A
3 B
4 C
5 A
6 C

Part 2
7 B
8 A
9 C
10 B
11 C
12 A
13 C

Part 3
14 A
15 C
16 A
17 C
18 B

Part 4
19 C
20 A
21 B
22 B
23 C
24 C

Part 5
25 in
26 have
27 The
28 it
29 Can/Could
30 of

Listening

Part 1
1 A
2 B
3 A
4 B
5 B

Part 2
6 4.45
7 15/fifteen
8 ticket
9 wallets
10 5819 236

Part 3
11 B
12 C
13 C
14 A
15 B

Part 4
16 C
17 C
18 A
19 A
20 B

Part 5
21 F
22 A
23 H
24 C
25 G

Model answers for Writing

These are the model answers for the Writing parts of Tests 1–8.

Test 1

Writing Part 6

Question 31

> Dear Jane,
> I hope you are well. Would you like to meet for lunch this weekend? What about on Saturday at 1 p.m.? We could eat at our usual cafe on the High Street.
> Best wishes,
> Belinda

Writing Part 7

Question 32

Tina packed her suitcase because she was going on a business trip. She got a taxi to the train station, but the traffic was very bad. Tina ran to catch the train, but she was too late and she missed it.

Test 2

Writing Part 6

Question 31

> Hi Paul,
> Would you like to go cycling on Saturday? We could cycle along the path around the lake. We can meet at the car park next to the lake.

Writing Part 7

Question 32

Last week, I packed my suitcase for a trip to London. When I arrived at the airport, I went to the check-in desk. However, I didn't have my passport. I didn't know where it was. Luckily, my sister found it at home and brought it to me at the airport.

Test 3

Writing Part 6

Question 31

> Hi Roger,
> Can you get me some fruit and vegetables when you go to the supermarket? I need five apples and two kilos of potatoes. I can pay you back this evening.
> Thanks very much.
> Jon

Writing Part 7

Question 32

One day some children were playing football. A large dog wanted to play with them. It joined their game, but it broke the ball. They children couldn't play football. After that, they played with the dog instead.

Test 4

Writing Part 6

Question 31

> Hi Peter,
> Let's meet at the underground station near the library on Wednesday. Shall we meet after the last class, around 3 p.m.? I'd like to borrow some books by British writers, and I hope you can help me find some good ones.

Writing Part 7

Question 32

Last week, my friend and I decided to go camping. We got our camping things ready and took our tents with us. When we arrived at the campsite, the weather changed. It was very windy and it started raining, so we couldn't make a campfire. In the end, we sat in our car and played card games.

Test 5

Writing Part 6

Question 31

> Hi Hannah,
> Would you like to come to my birthday party next week? It's on Friday evening at 7.00 p.m. at my flat. I will have snacks and a birthday cake, so you don't need to bring anything.

Writing Part 7

Question 32

One day a family went on a picnic. They found a place to sit, the children played and their parents put the food on the blanket. But the weather changed and it started to rain. The family ran to the car. They went to a restaurant for dinner. They were happy and they had a good time.

Test 6

Writing Part 6

Question 31

> Hi Amy,
> Let's play badminton at the sports centre in town on Saturday. We can meet there at half past ten. What would you like to do afterwards? How about going shopping at the new shopping centre?

Writing Part 7

Question 32

Yesterday, I wasn't feeling very well on my way to work. I had a headache and a temperature. When I got to work, I felt worse. My manager was worried about me and she told me to go home and rest. When I got home, I took some medicine, drank some water and went to bed.

Test 7

Writing Part 6

Question 31

> I'm so sorry I didn't come to the café on Friday. My mother got sick suddenly, so I went to see her. Would you like to meet tomorrow at eleven instead?
> Pippa

Writing Part 7

Question 32

One day a young woman wanted to read an article on her tablet. But she couldn't read it because she needed glasses. She went for an eye test and she bought some glasses. After that, she could read easily.

Test 8

Writing Part 6

Question 31

Hi Eddie,
I'm writing to say thank you for inviting me to stay at your house last weekend. I really enjoyed meeting your friends. They are a great group of people. I hope we can see each other again soon.
Yours,
Leslie

Writing Part 7

Question 32

One night a man wanted to go to sleep, but his neighbours were having a party. They were very noisy. He went next door and he asked them to be quiet. Then he went back to bed. It was quiet, so he went to sleep.

Model answers for Speaking

The model answers for the Speaking parts of Tests 1-8 are highlighted in grey here. You can listen to these model answers online at: www.collinselt.com/audio

Test 1

Speaking Part 1

06a

Examiner:	Good morning.
	Can I have your mark sheets, please?
	I'm Adam Brown. And this is Kate Mann.
	Candidate A, what's your name, please?
Candidate A:	My name's Melody Karra.
Examiner:	And Candidate B, what's your name, please?
Candidate B:	My name's Nicos Doukas.
Examiner:	Candidate B, do you work or are you a student?
Candidate B:	I'm a student.
Examiner:	Where do you live, Candidate B?
Candidate B:	I live in Piraeus.
Examiner:	Thank you.
	Candidate A, do you work or are you a student?
Candidate A:	I'm a student, too.
Examiner:	Where do you live?
Candidate A:	I live in Koukaki, in Athens.
Examiner:	Thank you.
Examiner:	Now, let's talk about family.
	Candidate A, when do you spend time with your family?
Candidate A:	I spend time with my family on Sundays. It's the day when we have a big meal together.
Examiner:	What do you like doing with your family?
Candidate A:	I like sitting around the table with my family and eating with them. And afterwards we often go for a walk.
Examiner:	Candidate B, who are your family members?
Candidate B:	I have two brothers and we live with my mother and father. I also have grandparents who live near us.
Examiner:	How much time do you spend with your family?
Candidate B:	We're all very busy, but we usually see each other in the evenings. And we also see each other at the weekend.
Examiner:	Now Candidate A, please tell me something about one person in your family.
Candidate A:	My sister is five years younger than me. She's always very happy and everyone loves her. She likes singing and dancing.
Examiner:	Now, let's talk about sport.
	Candidate B, how much sport do you play?
Candidate B:	I play a lot of sport and I really enjoy football, basketball and tennis.
Examiner:	Who do you play sport with, Candidate B?
Candidate B:	I play football with my friends and I'm in the local basketball team. I also play tennis with my brother when we have free time.
Examiner:	Candidate A, what sports are you good at?
Candidate A:	I'm not very good at them, but I like badminton.

Examiner:	When do you play sport?
Candidate A:	I don't play it very often, but when we go to the beach, I play badminton with my sister.
Examiner:	Now Candidate B, please tell me about your favourite sport.
Candidate B:	My favourite is football. I think it's the most exciting sport in the world. I play it twice a week and I also support my team, AEK Athens. I go to watch them play regularly.
Examiner:	Thank you.

Speaking Part 2

07a

Examiner:	Now, in this part of the test you are going to talk together. Here are some pictures that show different ways of travelling. Do you like these different ways of travelling? Say why or why not. I'll say that again. Do you like these different ways of travelling? Say why or why not. All right? Now, talk together.
Candidate A:	I think driving a car is a good way to travel. You can leave when you want to and go exactly where you want to. What do you think?
Candidate B:	Yes, I think you're right. If you have a car, your journey is very easy. You can get in your car at home and drive to where you want to go.
Candidate A:	What do you think about travelling by train?
Candidate B:	I think it's good to travel by train when you have to go on a long journey. If you want to go from one city to another, then a train is the best way to travel.
Candidate A:	I use the bus a lot in Athens. It's easy to catch the bus. I have a travel card so I don't have to pay every time.
Candidate B:	I don't think buses are very comfortable. They're usually very crowded and it can be difficult to find a seat.
Candidate A:	I don't think cycling is a very good idea in a big city. It can be dangerous when there's a lot of traffic. What do you think?
Candidate B:	I cycle to places near my home. But I agree with you. I don't like cycling on busy roads.
Candidate A:	Walking is a good way to travel if you don't have a long way to go. If the weather is fine, it can be nice. How do you feel about walking?
Candidate B:	I like walking. It's free, and it's good exercise, but it isn't very nice if the weather is bad.
Examiner:	Candidate A, do you think cars are a cheap way to travel?
Candidate A:	No, I don't.
Examiner:	Why?
Candidate A:	You have to buy a car, and a good car is expensive. You have to put petrol in it and petrol isn't cheap. You also need to repair it sometimes.
Examiner:	Candidate B, do you think cycling is fun?
Candidate B:	Yes. I like cycling. I have a bike and I use it a lot when I visit my friends and my grandparents.
Examiner:	So Candidate A, which of these ways of travelling do you like the most?
Candidate A:	I like travelling by car the most.
Examiner:	And you, Candidate B, which of these ways of travelling do you like the least?
Candidate B:	I like buses the least.
Examiner:	Thank you.
Examiner:	Now, would you prefer to walk or cycle, Candidate B?
Candidate B:	I'd prefer to cycle.
Examiner:	Why, Candidate B?
Candidate B:	It takes a long time to walk somewhere. Cycling is much quicker than walking.
Examiner:	And what about you, Candidate A? Would you prefer to travel by bus or by train?
Candidate A:	If I am going a long way, I prefer to travel by train. I think a train is more comfortable and you have more room on a train.
Examiner:	Do you think cars are safe, Candidate A?
Candidate A:	Yes, I do.

Examiner:	Why?
Candidate A:	If you are a careful driver, then a car is safe.
Examiner:	Do you think cars are safe, Candidate B?
Candidate B:	Not very safe. You can have an accident in a car. I think buses and trains are safer than cars.
Examiner:	Thank you. That is the end of the test.

Test 2

Speaking Part 1

13a

Examiner:	Good afternoon. Can I have your mark sheets, please? I'm Hannah Jones. And this is Keith Mantell. What's your name, Candidate A?
Candidate A:	My name's Andrea Chiti.
Examiner:	And what's your name, Candidate B?
Candidate B:	My name's Lucinda Fernandez.
Examiner:	Candidate B, do you work or are you a student?
Candidate B:	I'm a student.
Examiner:	Where do you come from, Candidate B?
Candidate B:	I'm from Barcelona in Spain.
Examiner:	Thank you. Candidate A, do you work or are you a student?
Candidate A:	I'm a student, too.
Examiner:	Where do you come from?
Candidate A:	I come from Rome in Italy.
Examiner:	Thank you.
Examiner:	Now, let's talk about jobs. Candidate A, what job would you like to have?
Candidate A:	I'm studying medicine at university, and one day I want to work as a doctor in a big hospital.
Examiner:	Why do you want to be a doctor?
Candidate A:	Because I think medicine is the most interesting subject to study, and I also want to help people.
Examiner:	Candidate B, what kinds of jobs do you think young people want to do?
Candidate B:	I think most young people want to do an interesting job. They would like to earn a good salary. I don't mean they want to become millionaires, but enough money to live well.
Examiner:	Would you like to work in an office, Candidate B?
Candidate B:	I'm not sure. But if the job is interesting and if the people are nice, why not?
Examiner:	Now Candidate A, please tell me something about a job that you wouldn't like to do.
Candidate A:	I wouldn't like to have a job in an office or a factory. I think it would be very boring, and a job in a factory is also very hard.
Examiner:	Now, let's talk about friends. Candidate B, how often do you see your friends?
Candidate B:	I see my friends every day during the break at college and usually every Saturday.
Examiner:	And Candidate B, what do you like doing with your friends?
Candidate B:	We're really into photography, so we enjoy walking around the city taking photos of people and buildings.
Examiner:	Candidate A, where do your friends live?

Model answers: Speaking

Candidate A: Most of my friends live in the same part of Rome as me and a few live in the countryside outside the city.

Examiner: When do you see your friends?

Candidate A: I usually don't get a chance to see my friends during the week, so I usually see them on Saturday or Sunday.

Examiner: Now Candidate B, please tell me something about one of your friends.

Candidate B: My best friend is Jordi. He's a student, like me, and he enjoys making videos about his hobby, which is doing graffiti, and uploading them to his blog.

Speaking Part 2

🎧
14a

Examiner: Now, in this part of the test you are going to talk together.
Here are some pictures that show different places to live.
Do you like these different places to live? Say why or why not. I'll say that again.
Do you like these different places to live? Say why or why not.
All right? Now, talk together.

Candidate A: I think it's nice to live in the apartment building and the house. How about you?

Candidate B: I like the apartment building, too, but I also like the houseboat.

Candidate A: Why do you like houseboats?

Candidate B: I think it would be really fun to live in a boat rather than a house. I live in a house now and it's not very exciting. If you live in a houseboat, you can travel to different places and still have all your own things with you. Why do you like the apartment building?

Candidate A: Well, I couldn't live on a farm or in a quiet village. In an apartment building, if you live at the top, you have great views!

Examiner: Candidate A, why do you think living in a house is nice?

Candidate A: Because houses usually have a garden and it's nice to have some outside space where you live.

Examiner: Candidate B, do you think living on a farm is fun?

Candidate B: No, I don't. I think it's really hard work to look after the animals, if you have them, and you have lots of things you need to take care of every day.

Examiner: So Candidate A, which of these places to live do you like best?

Candidate A: Well, if I have to choose between an apartment building and a house, I will choose the apartment building because they are usually in the centre of a town or city, so there are lots of shops, restaurants and interesting places to visit nearby.

Examiner: And you, Candidate B, which of these places to live do you like best?

Candidate B: I like houseboats the best. I think it would be fun in an apartment building in a city, but I think I would miss the open space outside. On a houseboat, you can enjoy being outdoors and you can also live in a really interesting home.

Examiner: Thank you.

Examiner: Now, do you prefer living in a big home or a small home, Candidate B?

Candidate B: I prefer living in a small home.

Examiner: Why, Candidate B?

Candidate B: Because it's easier to look after a small home and you don't have many rooms to clean. In a small home, you just have a few important pieces of furniture. I don't like places with a lot of things in them.

Examiner: And what about you, Candidate A? Do you prefer living in a big or small home?

Candidate A: I prefer a big home.

Examiner: Do you prefer living in cities or in the countryside, Candidate A?

Candidate A: I prefer living in cities because you have all the facilities you need, like shops, cafes, cinemas and parks.

Examiner: And you, Candidate B? Do you prefer living in cities or in the countryside?

Candidate B: I prefer living in the countryside.

Examiner:	Why is that, Candidate B?
Candidate B:	I like to be active and do lots of sports and outdoor activities like walking and cycling. I also prefer to live somewhere with fresh air and beautiful nature.
Examiner:	Thank you. That is the end of the test.

Test 3

Speaking Part 1

🎧
20a

Examiner:	Good morning.
	Can I have your mark sheets, please?
	I'm Keith Mantell. And this is Hannah Jones.
	Candidate A, what's your name, please?
Candidate A:	My name's Jakub Nowak.
Examiner:	And Candidate B, what's your name, please?
Candidate B:	My name's Yuki Takahashi.
Examiner:	Candidate B, do you work or are you a student?
Candidate B:	I work.
Examiner:	Where do you live, Candidate B?
Candidate B:	I'm from Tokyo, the capital city of Japan.
Examiner:	Thank you.
	Candidate A, do you work or are you a student?
Candidate A:	I'm a student.
Examiner:	Where do you come from?
Candidate A:	I come from Poznan, in Poland
Examiner:	Thank you.

Examiner:	Now, let's talk about holidays.
	Candidate A, how often do you go on holiday?
Candidate A:	I usually go on holiday once a year. We have a family holiday in the summer.
Examiner:	Where do you go on holiday?
Candidate A:	We often go to visit my grandparents. They live by the sea.
Examiner:	Candidate B, what kind of holidays do you like?
Candidate B:	I like beach holidays. I like swimming in the sea.
Examiner:	When do you take your holiday, Candidate B?
Candidate B:	Usually at the end of April, when most people take their holiday in Japan.

Examiner:	Now Candidate A, please tell me about a dream holiday you would like to take.
Candidate A:	I'd love to visit Florida for a holiday and see the Everglades. I'd also like to spend some time in Miami. I think it's an exciting place to visit. And of course, I'd also go to Disney World.

Examiner:	Now, let's talk about television.
	Candidate B, how often do you watch television?
Candidate B:	I don't watch it often because I'm very busy at work, so I don't have much free time.
Examiner:	What type of television programmes do you like, Candidate B?
Candidate B:	I like watching the news because I want to know what's going on in the world. I also enjoy watching quiz shows.
Examiner:	Candidate A, when do you watch television?
Candidate A:	I usually watch television in the evening when I want to relax. I like watching football, so if there's a big game on then I'll definitely watch television.
Examiner:	Who do you watch television with?
Candidate A:	If I watch late at night to relax, I watch it on my own, but when I watch football matches, I watch it with my friends.

Examiner:	Now Candidate B, please tell me about the sort of television programmes that you don't like.
Candidate B:	I don't like soap operas or reality shows. I think they're boring, so when they're on, I change the channel and watch something else. I also don't like watching sport.
Examiner:	Thank you.

Speaking Part 2

21a

Examiner:	Now, in this part of the test you are going to talk together. Here are some pictures that show different pets. Do you like these different pets? Say why or why not. I'll say that again. Do you like these different pets? Say why or why not. All right? Now, talk together.
Candidate A:	I think that a dog is a very good pet. What do you think?
Candidate B:	I agree. You can play with a dog and take it for walks. Also, a dog can be your friend.
Candidate A	What do you think about having a cat?
Candidate B:	I think cats are good pets, too. They're friendly, they sit with you and they keep you company. But sometimes they go out by themselves, so you might not see your cat for a long time.
Candidate A	I think fish are beautiful, especially colourful tropical fish, and watching them is relaxing.
Candidate B:	I don't think they're good pets. They're boring because they just swim round and round.
Candidate A:	I'm scared of snakes, so I don't think a snake is a good pet.
Candidate B:	I don't like them, either, and I don't think you can play with them. They aren't friendly and some snakes are dangerous.
Candidate A:	I don't think a bird is a good pet, either. I think it's cruel to keep birds in a cage. Do you like birds as pets?
Candidate B:	Not really, but some birds like parrots are very clever and they can learn to talk. So maybe they're good pets for old people.
Examiner:	Candidate A, do you think having a dog is fun?
Candidate A:	Yes, I do.
Examiner:	Why?
Candidate A:	You can take a dog anywhere with you. For example, you can play with it in the park or on the beach. You can throw things for it, like a ball, and you can have a lot of fun playing games with it.
Examiner:	Candidate B, do you think cats are fun?
Candidate B:	They're fun when they're young kittens and they're very cute. But they're not so much fun when they're older.
Examiner:	So Candidate A, which of these pets do you like the best?
Candidate A:	I like dogs the best.
Examiner:	And you, Candidate B, which of these pets do you like the best?
Candidate B:	I like cats.
Examiner:	Thank you.
Examiner:	Now, would you prefer a fish or a bird as a pet, Candidate B?
Candidate B:	I'd prefer a bird.
Examiner:	Why is that, Candidate B?
Candidate B:	Because birds are more interesting than fish. Some birds sing beautifully and some can sit on your hand. I think a bird can get to know you, but a fish can't.
Examiner:	And what about you, Candidate A? Would you prefer a fish or a bird as a pet?
Candidate A:	I'm not sure. I think I'd prefer a fish. Some fish are beautiful, and you can spend hours watching them. And I think they are easier to look after than birds.
Examiner:	Do you think pets are good for children, Candidate A?

Candidate A:	Yes, I do.
Examiner:	Why?
Candidate A:	Children can learn a lot from pets. They learn to look after them and they learn to be responsible.
Examiner:	Do you think pets are good for children, Candidate B?
Candidate B:	Yes, I agree with Candidate A. Most children like playing with pets. Also, I think it's good for them to learn about animals, how to feed them and make sure they are happy and healthy.
Examiner:	Thank you. That is the end of the test.

Test 4

Speaking Part 1

🎧
27a

Examiner:	Good morning.
	Can I have your mark sheets, please?
	I'm Lucy Clarke. And this is Richard Norton.
	What's your name, Candidate A?
Candidate A:	My name's Ling Li.
Examiner:	And what's your name, Candidate B?
Candidate B:	My name's Carlos Silva.
Examiner:	Candidate B, do you work or are you a student?
Candidate B:	I'm a student.
Examiner:	Where do you come from, Candidate B?
Candidate B:	I'm from São Paulo in Brazil.
Examiner:	Thank you.
	Candidate A, do you work or are you a student?
Candidate A:	I'm a student.
Examiner:	Where do you come from?
Candidate A:	I come from Beijing in China.
Examiner:	Thank you.
Examiner:	Now, let's talk about health and exercise.
	Candidate A, what do you do to stay healthy?
Candidate A:	I play badminton with my friends once a week and I also walk my dog in the park every morning. I try to eat lots of healthy food, like fruit and vegetables.
Examiner:	Do you get sick often?
Candidate A:	No, I don't get sick very often, usually a couple of times a year.
Examiner:	Candidate B, how often do you exercise?
Candidate B:	I exercise every day for about half an hour to an hour. I go for a run in the morning before college and I sometimes go swimming at my local swimming pool.
Examiner:	When was the last time you had to go to the doctor, Candidate B?
Candidate B:	I was there last month because I was feeling ill. I had a high temperature, a headache and a bad cough.
Examiner:	Now Candidate A, please tell me what you usually do when you don't feel well.
Candidate A:	I usually stay at home and rest. I either stay in bed or lie on the sofa and watch TV. I try to drink lots of water and my mum makes me soup.
Examiner:	Now, let's talk about technology.
	Candidate B, what types of technology do you use every day?
Candidate B:	I use my laptop every day. I take it with me in my backpack when I go to college so I can use it while I'm studying in the library.

Examiner:	What other technology is important to you in your everyday life, Candidate B?
Candidate B:	Well, my mobile phone is really important to me. I send a lot of messages to my friends or call them. I couldn't live without it.
Examiner:	Candidate A, is there a type of technology you couldn't live without?
Candidate A:	Yes, my digital camera. I study photography at college, so I take my camera with me everywhere. I have a camera on my mobile phone, too, of course, but I don't use it for my photography work.
Examiner:	How do you prefer to search for information when you are studying?
Candidate A:	I use the internet if I want to find something quickly, but I also go to the library and look for old photographs in books, magazines and journals.
Examiner:	Now Candidate B, please tell me if there is a time when you prefer not to use technology.
Candidate B:	In the evening, I switch off my phone an hour before I go to bed. I prefer to read a book to relax. Then I can sleep more easily.

Speaking Part 2

28a

Examiner:	Now, in this part of the test you are going to talk together. Here are some pictures that show different types of entertainment. Do you like these different types of entertainment? Say why or why not. I'll say that again. Do you like these different types of entertainment? Say why or why not. All right? Now, talk together.
Candidate A:	I like going to the cinema to watch the latest films. How about you?
Candidate B:	I enjoy playing video games at home.
Candidate A	Why do you like that?
Candidate B:	I like video games because they're really fun and a great way to relax. I usually play football or action games with my friends at the weekend. Also, if I'm feeling bored or have some free time I don't need to go out, I can just play some games. I'm really good at them, too. Why do you enjoy going to the cinema?
Candidate A	I like watching films because it's a good way to forget about your everyday life and worries for a few hours. Sometimes when I'm studying, I need a break, so I go to the cinema with my friends and it helps me relax for a while.
Examiner:	Candidate A, do you think going to an art exhibition is fun?
Candidate A:	Yes, I think it is. It's also interesting to see different types of art. Painting is one of my hobbies, and I sometimes go to art galleries to get ideas for my own work.
Examiner:	Candidate B, do you think going to the theatre is a pleasant way to spend an evening?
Candidate B:	Yes, I do, but it depends which theatre you go to. Some theatres have wonderful shows, like musicals, but the tickets are expensive, so I can't go often. But there are some small theatres, where you can watch really interesting plays – and the tickets are cheaper!
Examiner:	So Candidate A, which of these types of entertainment do you like the least?
Candidate A:	Well, I don't really like playing video games. I think they're boring and it isn't good for you to sit in front of a screen for many hours and not get any exercise.
Examiner:	And you, Candidate B, which of these types of entertainment do you like the least?
Candidate B:	I don't like going to music festivals because there are always too many people there. You can't get near the stage to see your favourite band. If you camp there, it's noisy at night, and if it rains, the grass gets very wet.
Examiner:	Thank you.
Examiner:	Now, do you prefer spending time with your friends and family or on your own, Candidate B?
Candidate B:	I like spending time with my friends and family, but sometimes I like to do things on my own.
Examiner:	Why is that, Candidate B?

Candidate B: My friends like doing the same activities as me, so we have fun together. I also love my family and I can talk to my parents and brother about anything. However, sometimes I like to relax and think by myself.

Examiner: And what about you, Candidate A? Do you prefer spending time with your friends and family or on your own?

Candidate A: Sometimes it's nice to do things with other people because it's more fun to do things together. And they can help you if you have any problems. But sometimes I also like to be by myself and read books or paint.

Examiner: Do you prefer indoor entertainment or having fun outdoors, Candidate A?

Candidate A: I prefer indoor entertainment, like going to the cinema, but I also enjoy going out and meeting new people. I meet lots of people like me when I go to art galleries.

Examiner: And you, Candidate B? Do you prefer entertainment inside or having fun outdoors?

Candidate B: I prefer having fun indoors, at home.

Examiner: Why is that, Candidate B?

Candidate B: Well, if I'm not playing video games, then I enjoying chatting to my friends online or watching TV. I'm not a very active person.

Examiner: Thank you. That is the end of the test.

Test 5

Speaking Part 1

34a

Examiner: Good afternoon.
Can I have your mark sheets, please?

I'm David Wheeler and this is Brenda Jones.
What's your name please, Candidate A?

Candidate A: My name's Adolfo da Silva.

Examiner: And what's your name please, Candidate B?

Candidate B: My name's Beatriz Costas.

Examiner: Candidate B, do you work or are you a student?

Candidate B: I'm a student.

Examiner: Where do you live, Candidate B?

Candidate B: I live in Benfica.

Examiner: Thank you.
Candidate A, do you work or are you a student?

Candidate A: I work.

Examiner: Where do you live?

Candidate A: I live in Alfama, south of the city centre.

Examiner: Thank you.

Examiner: Now, let's talk about food.
Candidate A, what is your favourite food?

Candidate A: I love my mother's food. She's a very good cook.

Examiner: What do you eat in the morning?

Candidate A: I usually have a cup of coffee with milk. I also have some toast with ham and cheese.

Examiner: Candidate B, what can you cook?

Candidate B: I can cook some simple dishes like pasta, but I'm not very good at cooking.

Examiner: And Candidate B what do you like to eat when you go to a restaurant?

Candidate B: I like to eat fish. Fish is very popular in my city.

Examiner: Now Candidate A, please tell me what you eat at home on a special day.

Candidate A: On special days I sit down with my family and we eat together. We always have a bean dish – we call it *feijoada* – with meat and fish. There is rice and bread to go with it.

Model answers: Speaking

Examiner:	Now, let's talk about shopping. Candidate B, what kind of shopping do you like?
Candidate B:	I like shopping for clothes and I often go shopping at the weekend.
Examiner:	Who do you go shopping with, Candidate B?
Candidate B:	I usually go with my sister and my friends, but sometimes I go with my mother.
Examiner:	Candidate A, do you prefer small local shops or big shops when you go shopping?
Candidate A:	I prefer going to the shopping centre with big shops.
Examiner:	How often do you go shopping?
Candidate A:	Not very often. I don't like it very much. I prefer to do other things.
Examiner:	Now Candidate B, please tell me about going shopping when you need clothes. Where do you go?
Candidate B:	If I need new clothes, I go to the shopping centre in the city centre. I go to lots of different shops and I try on different clothes. I take a long time to choose something!

Speaking Part 2

35a

Examiner:	Now, in this part of the test you are going to talk together. Here are some pictures that show different presents for a teenager. Do you like these different presents for a teenager? Say why or why not. I'll say that again. Do you like these different presents for a teenager? Say why or why not. All right? Now, talk together.
Candidate A:	I think a bicycle is a very good present. It's healthy for young people to go out on their bike. What do you think?
Candidate B:	Yes, I agree with you. It's fun to use and you can go to different places with your friends. What do you think about a laptop?
Candidate A	I think a laptop is a really good idea for a present for a teenager. I think a teenager would be very happy to get one. Do you agree?
Candidate B:	Yes, I do. The good thing about a laptop is that you can do lots of different things. You can study, you can play games and you can watch films.
Candidate A:	A mobile phone is a good present for an older teenager, but for a younger one, it might not be a good idea.
Candidate B:	But young teenagers love mobile phones. They want to talk to their friends all the time. But I think young children shouldn't spend too much time on a mobile.
Candidate A:	Now books, ... Hmm. I think a young teenager might think it's boring to get books.
Candidate B:	Yes, I think that's true for some people. But there are teenagers who really enjoy reading, and books are a good present for them.
Candidate A:	You're right. Now, a guitar. I think learning a musical instrument is a fun thing to do, so a guitar is a good idea for a present.
Candidate B:	Yes, I think so too. You can play music with other people if you learn to play the guitar, and maybe you can sing at the same time.
Examiner:	Candidate A, do you think a bicycle might be a dangerous present?
Candidate A:	Not really. If you are careful, then a bike is OK, but I think you should have lessons on how to cycle safely.
Examiner:	Candidate B, do you think some people might think a laptop is not a good present?
Candidate B:	Maybe. There are some bad things on the internet for young people, and sometimes people write horrible things on social media.
Examiner:	So Candidate A, which of these presents do you think is the best for a teenager?
Candidate A:	I think a bicycle is the best present.
Examiner:	And you, Candidate B, which of these presents do you think is the best?
Candidate B:	In my opinion a guitar is the best present.
Examiner:	Thank you.
Examiner:	Now, would you prefer a laptop or a mobile phone as a present, Candidate B?

Candidate B:	I'd prefer a phone.
Examiner:	Why is that, Candidate B?
Candidate B:	I'm very busy. I spend a lot of time away from my house. I walk a lot, I sit on the bus for a long time and I spend time at university. So I use a phone more than a laptop.
Examiner:	And what about you, Candidate A? Would you prefer books or a guitar for a present?
Candidate A:	I'd prefer a guitar. I can get books from the library, but I've never played a musical instrument, and I'd like to try.
Examiner:	Do you like cycling, Candidate A?
Candidate A:	Yes, I do.
Examiner:	Why?
Candidate A:	It's quick and easy to get somewhere. But it's not good if it's raining.
Examiner:	Do you like reading, Candidate B?
Candidate B:	Not really. For me, reading is like work. I have to read a lot when I study, so I want to do something different when I relax.
Examiner:	Thank you. That is the end of the test.

Test 6

Speaking Part 1

41a

Examiner:	Good evening.
	Can I have your mark sheets, please?
	I'm Valerie Walker. And this is James Liddell.
	What's your name, Candidate A?
Candidate A:	My name's Vittoria Conti.
Examiner:	And what's your name, Candidate B?
Candidate B:	My name's Rasmus Tamm.
Examiner:	Candidate B, do you work or are you a student?
Candidate B:	I work.
Examiner:	Where do you come from, Candidate B?
Candidate B:	I'm from Tallinn in Estonia.
Examiner:	Thank you.
	Candidate A, do you work or are you a student?
Candidate A:	I'm a student.
Examiner:	Where do you come from?
Candidate A:	I come from Lugano in Switzerland.
Examiner:	Thank you.
Examiner:	Now, let's talk about hobbies.
	Candidate A, what hobbies do you do during the week?
Candidate A:	One of my hobbies is music. I play the guitar in a band, and I usually practise every evening after college.
Examiner:	What activities did you do last weekend?
Candidate A:	I went camping with some friends at the weekend. We stayed in tents at a campsite in the forest. We often go camping there because we hike in the mountains.
Examiner:	Candidate B, what hobbies do you have?
Candidate B:	I'm very interested in art, especially modern art, and I enjoy going to museums and art galleries with my friends.
Examiner:	How often are you able to do this, Candidate B?
Candidate B:	In the week, I am very busy at work, so I can't go to museums. I usually go at the weekend.
Examiner:	Now Candidate A, please tell me something about what activities you like to do with your family.

Model answers: Speaking

Candidate A: At the weekend I like to go cycling with my brother. My family and I also enjoy having barbecues on a Saturday afternoon if the weather is nice.

Examiner: Now, let's talk about clothes.
                 Candidate B, what clothes do you wear every day?
Candidate B: I wear trousers, a jacket, a shirt and tie to work. If it's cold, I also wear a jumper or a coat.
Examiner: And Candidate B what colours do you like for clothes?
Candidate B: I like wearing blue or black in the winter, but in the summer, I wear lighter colours. And I like wearing colourful shirts.
Examiner: Candidate A, what clothes do you wear when you go to a party?
Candidate A: I usually wear a dress, a jacket and smart shoes. I also sometimes wear trousers with a blouse.
Examiner: How often do you buy clothes?
Candidate A: I usually buy clothes once a month when I go shopping with my friends. If I need something, I'll buy it sooner. I try not to buy clothes very often.

Examiner: Now Candidate B, please tell me something about the clothes you like to buy.
Candidate B: I like fashion, so I often buy clothes that I see in magazines and online. I like buying jeans, T-shirts and trainers.

Speaking Part 2

42a

Examiner: Now, in this part of the test you are going to talk together.
                 Here are some pictures that show different outdoor activities.
                 Do you like these different outdoor activities? Say why or why not. I'll say that again.
                 Do you like these different outdoor activities? Say why or why not.
                 All right? Now, talk together.
Candidate A: I like a few of these. I like to be active and go outside with my friends so I've done many of these activities. How about you?
Candidate B: I'm not a fan of most of these types of activities because I'm not very good at sport. I've never tried skateboarding and I don't like golf or swimming in lakes. I sometimes go swimming at the sports centre because the pool is inside and it's warmer.
Candidate A   Do you ever have picnics in the park?
Candidate B: Sometimes, at the beach in summer, but I don't live near any nice parks, so I don't have picnics in parks. How about you?
Candidate A   I really enjoy having picnics and eating outside with my family or friends. We usually take food with us in a basket when we go walking in the countryside. When we find a nice place, we sit and eat our food.
Examiner: Candidate A, do you think skateboarding is difficult?
Candidate A: Yes, I think it is. I tried skateboarding when I was younger, but I kept falling off. I think that if you don't wear safety clothes, you could hurt yourself.
Examiner: Candidate B, do you think swimming in a lake is dangerous?
Candidate B: Yes, I think it can be because a lake is big and if you swim out too far, it might be difficult to swim back again.
Examiner: So Candidate A, what do you think of music festivals?
Candidate A: I don't like them. They're noisy and there are too many people. I prefer going to concerts indoors.
Examiner: And you, Candidate B, do you think going to music festivals is fun?
Candidate B: Yes, I do. I enjoy watching my favourite bands and singers on stage and listening to live music. I enjoy singing along with everyone else in the audience, too.
Examiner: Candidate A, which of these activities do you like best?
Candidate A: I think swimming in the lake is the best outdoor activity because it's good exercise. I enjoy swimming and I love to be close to nature.
Examiner: And you, Candidate B, which of these activities do you like best?

Candidate B:	I think going to music festivals is the best outdoor activity because you can listen to your favourite music and dance with your friends.
Examiner:	Thank you.
Examiner:	Now, do you prefer being by the sea or in the mountains, Candidate B?
Candidate B:	I like being by the sea.
Examiner:	Why is that, Candidate B?
Candidate B:	Because it's relaxing. You can sit on the beach and read a book in the warm sun. It's usually quiet on the beach near my house, so I can listen to the birds, smell the sea air and forget about any problems.
Examiner:	And what about you, Candidate A? Do you prefer being by the sea or in the mountains?
Candidate A:	I prefer being in the mountains because there is lots of fresh air. I enjoy hiking and exploring the forests and looking at wildlife.
Examiner:	Is it better to do sports alone or with other people, Candidate A?
Candidate A:	I think it's better to do sports with other people. I like playing team sports because it's more fun to work together to win. I think it's important to spend time with other people.
Examiner:	And you, Candidate B? Is it better to do sports alone or with other people?
Candidate B:	I don't often play sports because I'm not very good at them. When I go to the gym, I prefer to exercise alone. I don't like big exercise classes.
Examiner:	Why?
Candidate B:	When I exercise, I have time to think. I think about my job and the future. I don't like to exercise and chat at the same time.
Examiner:	Thank you. That is the end of the test.

Test 7

Speaking Part 1

48a

Examiner:	Good morning.
	Can I have your mark sheets, please?
	I'm Jack Rider. And this is Linda Smith.
	Candidate A, what's your name, please?
Candidate A:	My name's Chiara Bianchi.
Examiner:	And Candidate B, what's your name, please?
Candidate B:	I'm Matteo Romano.
Examiner:	Candidate B, do you work or are you a student?
Candidate B:	I'm a student.
Examiner:	Where do you live, Candidate B?
Candidate B:	I live in Naples.
Examiner:	Thank you.
	Candidate A, do you work or are you a student?
Candidate A:	I'm a student.
Examiner:	Where do you live?
Candidate A:	I also live in Naples. In Soccavo, in the west of the city.
Examiner:	Thank you.
Examiner:	Now, let's talk about the weather.
	Candidate A, what is the weather like in the summer where you live?
Candidate A:	It's really hot in Naples in the summer. It's often over 31 or 32 degrees, so you can't stay in the sun for a long time.
Examiner:	What about the winter?
Candidate A:	It doesn't often get very cold, and it almost never snows.

Model answers: Speaking

Examiner:	Candidate B, what sort of weather do you like?
Candidate B:	I like it when it's not too hot and not too cold, so I like the spring and the autumn. It's nice when it's sunny and you can go out and do activities outside.
Examiner:	What do you do when the weather is good, Candidate B?
Candidate B:	I play football with my friends. If it's a Sunday, then my family and I have lunch on the balcony, or we have a picnic, or eat outside at a restaurant.
Examiner:	Now Candidate A, please tell me what sort of weather you don't like.
Candidate A:	I don't like it when it rains. I hate getting wet. It's worse when it's windy as well. Then you can't use an umbrella and everything gets wet. When my hair gets wet, it looks terrible!
Examiner:	Now, let's talk about school. Candidate B, what was your school like?
Candidate B:	It was very good. It was a big, modern school, the teachers were excellent, and I had lots of friends.
Examiner:	What was your favourite subject, Candidate B?
Candidate B:	I liked my English classes because we did lots of interesting activities in class.
Examiner:	Candidate A, what did you like about your school?
Candidate A:	We had a friendly head teacher. She helped everyone to do their best.
Examiner:	Was there anything you didn't like about your school?
Candidate A:	We always had a lot of homework and I didn't like doing it, especially at the weekend and in the evenings.
Examiner:	Now Candidate B, please tell me about a good teacher that you can remember from school.
Candidate B:	I can remember my maths teacher. His name was Signor Ricci. He was very patient with us. He never got angry and he always explained things carefully. Everybody liked him and learned from him.

Speaking Part 2

49a

Examiner:	Now, in this part of the test you are going to talk together. Here are some pictures that show different jobs. Do you like these different jobs? Say why or why not. I'll say that again. Do you like these different jobs? Say why or why not. All right? Now, talk together.
Candidate A:	I think a teacher is a good job because you can help young children learn. This is very important. What do you think about being a teacher?
Candidate B:	I think teaching is a good job too. It's important because you guide young people and help them understand difficult subjects.
Candidate A	What do you think about being a cook?
Candidate B:	I think being a cook is hard work. Cooks work long hours, and it's very hot in the kitchen. There's a lot of work to do, so I don't think I'd like to be a cook.
Candidate A:	I agree. But I think a dentist is a good job and it's also useful. Everybody needs dentists.
Candidate B:	I agree with you. And I think dentists can earn a lot of money so that's another reason why it's a good job.
Candidate A:	I'm not sure about a firefighter. What do you think about that?
Candidate B:	I think a firefighter could be a dangerous job. But it's another very useful job and we need people to fight fires.
Candidate A:	The last job is a mechanic. I don't think I'd like to be one. It's a hard job and you get very dirty when you work with cars all day.

Candidate B:	I think if you have your own business it could be very good. But it might not be so good if you work for somebody else.
Examiner:	Candidate A, do you think being a dentist is interesting?
Candidate A:	Yes, I do.
Examiner:	Why?
Candidate A:	You meet different people. Also, everybody's teeth are different, so you see something different every day. It's never boring.
Examiner:	Candidate B, do you think being a cook is interesting?
Candidate B:	No, I don't think it's very interesting. You have to be in a kitchen all the time and you have to cook the same food from the menu.
Examiner:	So Candidate A, which of these jobs do you like the best?
Candidate A:	I think being a dentist is the best job.
Examiner:	And you, Candidate B, which of these jobs do you like the best?
Candidate B:	I think a teacher is the best job.
Examiner:	Thank you.
Examiner:	Now, Candidate B, which job do you think is better, a mechanic or a firefighter?
Candidate B:	I think a firefighter is a better job.
Examiner:	Why is that, Candidate B?
Candidate B:	Because you go to different places to fight fires. A mechanic has to go to work in the same place every day and he – or she – works on cars all the time.
Examiner:	And what about you, Candidate A? Which job do you think is better, a cook or a firefighter?
Candidate A:	I think a cook is a better job than a firefighter. A cook can sometimes prepare new dishes. When you are a firefighter, you have to be ready to go to work at any time because a fire can start in the middle of the night.
Examiner:	Which job do you think is the worst job, Candidate A?
Candidate A:	Being a mechanic.
Examiner:	Why?
Candidate A:	I don't think it's interesting and you get very dirty.
Examiner:	What do you think is the worst job, Candidate B?
Candidate B:	For me, being a cook is the worst because I'm a terrible cook and I don't like cooking. I'm not patient enough. I like eating, not cooking.
Examiner:	Thank you. That is the end of the test.

Test 8

Speaking Part 1

55a

Examiner:	Good afternoon. Can I have your mark sheets, please? I'm Anita Hill. And this is Mark Flock. Candidate A, what's your name, please?
Candidate A:	My name's Emir Yilmaz.
Examiner:	And Candidate B, what's your name, please?
Candidate B:	My name's Zeynap Ozturk.
Examiner:	Candidate B, do you work or are you a student?
Candidate B:	I'm a student.
Examiner:	And where do you live, Candidate B?
Candidate B:	I live in Goztepe.
Examiner:	Thank you. Candidate A, do you work or are you a student?
Candidate A:	I'm a student.
Examiner:	Where do you live?

Candidate A:	I live in Goztepe, too. It is an area next to Kadikoy.
Examiner:	Thank you.

Examiner:	Now, let's talk about music. Candidate A, are you a musical person?
Candidate A:	I'm not sure! I think I'm musical, but my family say I've got a terrible voice! However, I love listening to pop music on the radio.
Examiner:	Do you like music from your country?
Candidate A:	To be honest, traditional Turkish music is not my favourite. I like it, but I like Western pop music more.
Examiner:	Candidate B, what sort of music do you like?
Candidate B:	I like lots of different types of music. I like singing traditional Turkish songs. But I like modern singers too.
Examiner:	When do you listen to music, Candidate B?
Candidate B:	I listen to music every day. I download music on my phone and I listen to it when I am travelling to university. I also listen to music at home.

Examiner:	Now Candidate A, please tell me about a musical instrument you play or you would like to play.
Candidate A:	I'd like to play the guitar. My friend has one and he plays it well. It sounds really good and I wish I could play it too.

Examiner:	Now, let's talk about studying. Candidate B, where do you usually study?
Candidate B:	I usually go to the library at university to study. It's very quiet. I can stay there for hours and no one bothers me.
Examiner:	Do you always study on your own, Candidate B?
Candidate B:	Yes, I do. I don't like studying with other people because they often talk about other things and waste time.
Examiner:	Candidate A, do you study a lot online?
Candidate A:	Yes, I do. I find articles to read online and I like writing online because I can save my work easily.
Examiner:	Are there any disadvantages to studying online?
Candidate A:	Yes, if you aren't careful, you start to do other things instead of studying. For example, talking to your friends on social media.

Examiner:	Now Candidate B, please tell me how you feel about going to class with other students and listening to a teacher. Do you think that is a good way to study and to learn things?
Candidate B:	I think it can be a good way to learn, but it depends on the teacher. If the teacher is boring, the students don't pay attention and they don't learn, but if the teacher is good, then I think it's the best way to learn.

Speaking Part 2

🎧
56a

Examiner:	Now, in this part of the test you are going to talk together. Here are some pictures that show different ways of getting the news. Do you like these different ways of getting the news? Say why or why not. I'll say that again. Do you like these different ways of getting the news? Say why or why not. All right? Now, talk together.
Candidate A:	I think a newspaper is an old-fashioned way of reading the news. What do you think?
Candidate B:	Yes, I agree with you. I think it's for older people who have a lot of time because there's a lot to read in a newspaper.
Candidate A	What do you think about watching the news on television?

Candidate B:	I think it's a good way to get the news. The news on television is good quality, and you know that the stories are true.
Candidate A:	I agree. You can also read about the news on your phone. A lot of people get news on their phone through apps, but I don't think it's easy to read stories on a small screen.
Candidate B:	Yes, that's right, and some of the news may not be very good quality. I think there's a lot of fake news on the internet.
Candidate A:	What do you think about reading the news on a laptop?
Candidate B:	I think it's a good way. It's up to date and you can read longer articles more easily because the screen is bigger than a phone screen. You can play videos too.
Candidate A:	Finally, the radio. I never listen to the news on the radio. What about you?
Candidate B:	Not really. I use it to listen to music and football, but I don't use it to hear the news.
Examiner:	Candidate A, do you think newspapers are interesting?
Candidate A:	No, I don't.
Examiner:	Why not?
Candidate A:	It isn't up to date because the news in it is from the day before. It takes a long time to get the newspaper to the shop and for someone to buy it. So when you read it, it's already old.
Examiner:	Candidate B, do you think the news on the radio is interesting?
Candidate B:	No, I don't. I think it's boring because you can only listen to it and you can't see any pictures or videos.
Examiner:	So Candidate A, which of these ways of getting the news do you like the best?
Candidate A:	I think using a mobile phone is the best way. The screen is small, but you always have your phone with you, so you can look at it when you want.
Examiner:	And you, Candidate B, which of these ways do you like the best?
Candidate B:	I think a laptop is the best way to find out what is going on in the news.
Examiner:	Thank you.
Examiner:	Now, Candidate B, can you compare getting the news on the television with getting the news on the radio?
Candidate B:	I think they're similar ways. You have to wait for the news programme to start, so they're different from other ways of getting the news. You can read a newspaper or get the news online whenever you want.
Examiner:	And what about you, Candidate A? Can you compare getting the news on a phone with getting the news on a laptop?
Candidate A:	I think these are similar ways of getting the news. The difference is that you can carry your phone and look at it when you want, so you can get the news all the time, for example, when you're sitting on the bus.
Examiner:	Which of these ways of getting the news is least useful to you?
Candidate A:	Reading a newspaper.
Examiner:	Why?
Candidate A:	As I said before, the news is old. You have to read it, so it's harder than listening or watching.
Examiner:	What do you think is the least useful way to get the news, Candidate B?
Candidate B:	For me, the radio is the least useful. If I have time I might read a newspaper, but I never listen to the radio. I prefer to follow the news on my laptop so I can choose the stories that I'm interested in.
Examiner:	Thank you. That is the end of the test.

Speaking: Additional practice by topic

This section will give you extra practice in the sorts of questions the examiner may ask you in Part 1 of the Speaking test. Listen to the audio and practise answering the questions. Some of the questions are similar but the words used in the question are different; this gives you more speaking practice and shows you how different questions are formed. Remember that the examiner will choose what questions to ask you and won't ask you lots of questions about the same topic.

When you are practising try to give a longer answer, even if you want to just say *No*. For example, you may not like doing sport, but if the question is *Do you like playing tennis?* and your real answer is *No*, you can say something like *No, I don't like playing tennis because I didn't learn how to play it when I was at school*.

Once you are feeling confident it would be a good idea not to look at the book – just listen to the audio and answer the questions. And keep practising!

The questions are grouped under different topic headings: books and films; clothes and accessories; communication and technology; education; family and friends; food; health and exercise; hobbies and interests; house and home; personal feelings and experiences; places in a town, a city and the countryside; shopping; sport; the natural world and weather; travel and transport; work and jobs.

Books and films

57
Now let's talk about books and films.
Tell us about what books you like to read.
Do you like reading?
Do you read many books?
What books do you read the most?
What is your favourite type of book?
Do you read books online?
Do you like to read comic books? Why/why not?
Do you prefer to read a book or watch a film?
Are you a fan of watching films? Why/why not?
What films do you like to watch?
What was the last film you saw?
How often do you go to the cinema?
Is there a cinema near where you live?
Do you enjoy going to the cinema?
Who do you go to the cinema with?
Do you enjoy watching films at home?
Are there any films you dislike?
Is there a film you want to see?
Who is your favourite actor?

Clothes and accessories
58
Now let's talk about clothes and accessories.
Tell us about the clothes and accessories you wear every day.
What clothes do you wear at the weekend?
What clothes do you have to wear to work?
Have you ever worn a uniform? When?
What clothes do you wear when you exercise?
Where do you like to buy clothes?
What type of clothes do you not like to wear?
What did you wear last weekend?
What clothes do you wear at a party?
Are you interested in the clothes other people wear?

What types of clothes do your friends wear?
What do you like to wear in hot weather?
Do you like to wear jewellery?
Do you like to shop in department stores?

Communication and technology

Now let's talk about communication and technology.
Tell us about what technology you use every day.
How often do you buy new technology?
What technology do you use the most?
Tell us how you like to talk to your family and friends.
Do you talk to your friends online?
What do you like talking about with your friends?
When was the last time you spoke with a friend on the phone?
Do you think it's better to write messages to your friends or chat to them on the phone?
Do you watch films online?
What websites do you often use?
Do you like to take photos with your smartphone?
How often do you watch TV?
Do you prefer using a computer or a laptop? Why?
How do you like listening to music?
Do you listen to the radio online?

Education

Now let's talk about education.
Tell us about what you studied at school.
Did you like school when you were younger?
What was your favourite subject?
Who was your favourite teacher at school?
How often do you study English every week?
What time of day do you like to study?
Where do you prefer to study?
Do you like to study with other people or on your own?
Do you ever study online?
Do you find learning English easy or difficult? Why?
Do you think learning is important? Why?
What subject would you like to study?

Family and friends

Now let's talk about family and friends.
Tell us about your family.
Who do you live with?
Do you have any brothers or sisters?
Where does your family live?
Is there anyone in your family who is especially important to you? Why?
What activities do you like to do with your family?
What do you enjoy doing most together with your family?
Tell us about your friends.
Do you live near your friends?
How often do you see your friends?
What do you like to do together with your friends?
Do you have the same hobbies as any of your friends? What are they?
Do you think having friends is important? Why?
Did you see any of your friends at the weekend?
How do you like to chat with your friends?

Food

62

Now let's talk about food.
Tell us about something you ate yesterday.
What time do you usually eat breakfast?
What do you like to eat for lunch?
When do you eat dinner?
What do you like to eat after college/work?
What is your favourite food?
How often do you eat at a restaurant?
What is your favourite place to eat?
Do you ever go on picnics? What food do you take with you?
Who cooks the meals in your home?
Who do you like to cook for?
Are you good at cooking? What do you like to cook?
What types of food do you like to eat?
Is there any food you dislike? What is it?
What food do you like to eat with friends?

Health and exercise

63

Now let's talk about health and exercise.
Tell us about what you do to be healthy.
How often do you visit the doctor's?
When was the last time you were ill?
What do you do when you're not feeling well?
What healthy foods do you eat?
Do you drink a lot of water?
How often do you exercise?
What type of sport do you play?
Do you like to go to the gym?
Do you prefer to exercise alone or with friends?
How often do you walk?
How many hours of exercise do you do every week?
What exercise do you do at the weekend?
Are there types of exercise you dislike?
Have you ever taken part in a sports competition? What was it?

Hobbies and interests

64

Now let's talk about hobbies and interests.
Tell us about your hobbies and interests.
What hobbies do you have?
What hobbies did you have when you were younger?
Do you enjoy doing any hobbies with friends?
Is there a hobby you'd like to try?
What do you like to do in the evenings?
What do you like to do at the weekends?
Do you prefer to do activities alone or with other people?
What are the most popular hobbies where you live?
Are there any hobbies that you dislike? What are they?
What do you do when you get home from your studies or work?
How often do you play sport?
Have you ever been camping? When? Did you like it?
Do you play any instruments? What do you play?
Do you enjoying taking photos?

How often do you visit a museum?
What time of year do you go on holiday?
Do you like singing or dancing? Why/why not?
How often do you ride a bike?

House and home

Now let's talk about house and home.
Tell us about where you live.
Where do you live?
What is your home like?
Is your home new or old?
What rooms do you have in your home?
What do you like about where you live?
What is your favourite place in your home?
What furniture do you have in your house?
Do you live with anyone?
What do you dislike about where you live?
Is your home near your family or friends' homes?
How would you describe your home?
Where do you relax in your home?
What do you do when you get home in the evenings?
Is there anything you'd like to change about your home?

Personal feelings and experiences

Now let's talk about feelings and experiences.
Tell us about what makes you happy.
What is important in your life?
What makes you feel worried?
What was the last thing you did that scared you?
Is there anything you are afraid of?
What is the best experience of your life so far?
Is there anything you find boring?
What do you find interesting?
What is the worst experience of your life?
What do you find difficult?
How do you celebrate your birthday?
What is your favourite time of the year?
Tell us about a time when you were brave.
What makes you angry?

Places in a town, a city and the countryside

Now let's talk about places in a town, a city or the countryside.
Tell us about the place where you live.
Do you prefer to live in the town, city or countryside?
What types of places do you have where you live?
Tell us about what the countryside is like near where you live.
Do you live near the sea or mountains?
Do you have any farms near where you live?
How far away do you live from an airport?
What interesting places do you have in your town/city?
Are there any busy roads where you live?
Do you live far from the place where you study or work?
What is the most beautiful area where you live?

Do people visit your town/city on holiday? Where do they go?
Do you live near the beach?
Do you have any good restaurants or cafes where you live?
What buildings are there in your town/city?

Shopping

68

Now let's talk about shopping.
Tell us about what shops you often go to.
How often do you go shopping?
What shops do you have where you live?
Where is your nearest supermarket?
Do you ever go shopping in department stores?
Do you like to try on clothes when you go shopping?
Who do you go shopping with?
How do you like to pay in a shop?
Do you ask for help from the shop assistant when you go shopping?
Do you prefer to go shopping alone or with other people?
Do you like shopping when there are sales?
What things do you buy every week?
Are the shops where you live cheap or expensive?
Do you take your own bags when you go shopping or do you use plastic bags?
Do you like shopping? Why or why not?

Sport

69

Now let's talk about sport.
Tell us about the sports you like.
What sport do you play every week?
Is there a sport that you dislike?
What sport did you play when you were younger?
Is there a sport that you aren't good at?
Are you a fan of any sports teams or players?
Do you watch sport on TV?
Do you prefer to play sport inside or outside?
What sports do you think are dangerous?
Have you ever entered a sports competition?
Were you a member of a sports team when you were younger?
How often do you go swimming?
What clothes do you wear when you play sport?
Have you ever won any sports prizes?
Have you ever tried any water sports? What did you try? Did you enjoy it?

The natural world and weather

70

Now let's talk about the natural world and the weather.
Tell us about your favourite season.
What weather do you often have where you live?
What's the weather like in spring where you live?
What's the weather like in autumn where you live?
Tell us about what nature you have where you live.
Does the weather ever get very hot where you live?
What activities do you do when the weather is cold?
What types of animals do you have where you live?
Do you think it's important to take care of nature?
Do you grow any plants or trees where you live?

What's your favourite type of weather?
Do you live near the countryside? What is it like?
What natural places do people enjoy visiting in your country?

Travel and transport

71

Now let's talk about travel and transport.
Tell us about how you travel every day.
What transport do you often use?
What transport do you dislike using?
What is the fastest way to get around where you live?
Do you think it's better to walk or get the bus?
What do you think of the transport where you live?
How do people who visit your country travel around?
Have you ever travelled by train? Where did you go?
How do you prefer to travel every day?
Is the transport good or bad where you live? Why?
Do you have many visitors travelling to your country?
Do you drive? When did you learn?
How often do you travel on the motorways where you live?
How many airports do you have where you live?
Do you like to travel by plane?

Work and jobs

72

Now let's talk about work and jobs.
Tell us about what jobs you have done.
What was your first job?
What would you like to be doing in ten years?
Are there any jobs you wouldn't want to do?
What things at work or at your job are you good at?
What is your dream job?
What is your worst job?
Do people have to wear uniforms at work where you live?
What clothes do you wear to work?
Is it easy or difficult to get a job where you live?
What is the place like where you work?
Is there any place you'd like to work in?
What job did you want to do when you were younger?